Jumpstart Your *New* Business *Now!*

The Entrepreneur's Guide to Starting & Growing a Profitable Business Doing What You Love

2nd Edition

By Katrina Sawa

CEO & Founder of
JumpstartYourBizNow.com,
and JumpstartPublishing.net

Jumpstart
PUBLISHING

Copyright © 2023 by Katrina Sawa and K. Sawa Marketing International Inc. All rights reserved. No part of this book or its associated ancillary materials may be reproduced or transmitted in any form or by any means, electronic or mechanical, including photocopying, recording, or by any informational storage or retrieval system without permission from the publisher.

Published by K. Sawa Marketing International Inc., D.B.A. Jumpstart Publishing PO Box 6, Roseville, CA 95661. (916) 872-4000 www.JumpstartPublishing.net

DISCLAIMER AND/OR LEGAL NOTICES

While all attempts have been made to verify information provided in this book and its ancillary materials, neither the author or publisher assumes any responsibility for errors, inaccuracies, or omissions and is not responsible for any financial loss by customer in any manner. Any slights of people or organizations are unintentional. If advice concerning legal, financial, accounting or related matters is needed, the services of a qualified professional should be sought. This book and its associated ancillary materials, including verbal and written training, is not intended for use as a source of legal, financial or accounting advice.

EARNINGS & INCOME DISCLAIMER

With respect to the reliability, accuracy, timeliness, usefulness, adequacy, completeness, and/or suitability of information provided in this book, Katrina Sawa, K. Sawa Marketing International Inc., its partners, associates, affiliates, consultants, and/or presenters make no warranties, guarantees, representations, or claims of any kind. Readers' results will vary depending on a number of factors. Any and all claims or representations as to income earnings are not to be considered as average earnings. Testimonials are not representative. This book and all products and services are for educational and informational purposes only. You agree that Katrina Sawa and/or K. Sawa Marketing International Inc. is not responsible for the success or failure of your business, personal, health or financial decisions relating to any information presented by Katrina Sawa, K. Sawa Marketing International Inc., or company products/services. Earnings potential is entirely dependent on the efforts, skills and application of the individual person.

Any examples, stories, reference, or case studies are for illustrative purposes only and should not be interpreted as testimonies and/or examples of what reader and/or consumers can generally expect from the information. No representation in any part of this information, materials and/or seminar training are guarantees or promised for actual performance. Any statements, strategies, concepts, techniques, exercises and ideas in the information, materials and/or seminar training offered are simply opinion or experience, and thus should not be misinterpreted as promises, typical results or guarantees (expressed or implied). This book is provided "as is," and without warranties.

ISBN: 978-1-7358666-6-6

PRINTED IN THE UNITED STATES OF AMERICA

Praise for the book, Jumpstart Your New Business Now

"Katrina presents a very straightforward and pragmatic approach for BEING successful in business. She knows her stuff and has taken the time to integrate all of the tips and tools you need to love your life and your work. Katrina enjoys supporting individuals who are interested in taking their business seriously. No matter where you are in business, or in life, you will find a sweet nugget in Jumpstart Your New Business Now!" – Dr. Deborah Hrivnak

"I love how Katrina gives us what we need to know and shares how we can prepare to be successful in our businesses. There are so many things that entrepreneurs NEED to know when starting a business, Katrina is your go-to resource to get started the RIGHT way so that you can avoid setbacks and set yourself up for success. Be sure to highlight the nuggets of knowledge in the book!" – Carey McLean, The App Chicks

"Katrina has solid business experience that she gladly gives to all who talk to her. This book is a must buy for anyone looking to start or uplevel their business. She gives you the blueprint to being successful. Buy the book, read the book and then *follow her advice. You will be glad you did!"* – Kim McLaughlin, Emotional Eating Coach and Speaker

"Great resource for entrepreneurs! Wonderful insights and tips for getting your business going and growing it into a business you love!" – Terry V. Broadbent

"Katrina Sawa knows her stuff--and this book is filled with "aha moments". I especially loved her line, "I say charge as much as you possibly can without stuttering." Love it!" – Donald E. Franceschi, Author of the book, From Awful to Awesome, 9 Essential Tools for Effective Presentations

"Fantastic book! Katrina's Jumpstart book is filled with priceless information that is practical and works." – Dusti Garside-Branecki, Your Housekeeping Fairy Godmother

"Great book that takes you through a step-by-step process to either start your business or expand the one you already have. It is like having Katrina holding your hand through the entire process. This book challenges you to think bigger while keeping it realistic and shows you how to create a step-by-step plan to achieve your goals. Great hands-on exercises and free resources on her website as well. If you are struggling and overwhelmed trying to figure out how

to get your business started...stop it and go buy this book now!" – Leslie Lajes

"Katrina Sawa is the person I turn to for business and marketing advice. I knew instantly I needed to buy her book because of the incredible and valuable insight she has into the business world. If you own a business or thought about starting one, you must first buy this book." – Sean Douglas, Motivational Speaker & Podcast Host

"If you want a business coach in your corner really supporting you and your business, I highly recommend Katrina and her new book." – Matt Brauning, Motivational Speaker and Podcast Host

"I have worked with Katrina in the past and she is absolutely amazing. Her many years of experience has helped launch my career as a Mindset Coach. The Entrepreneur's Guide is a must read. Katrina provides useful tools and tips to help launch your business! Great work Katrina!" – Megan Fenyoe

"Whether you are in the planning phase to start up a business, or if you have been in business for a while & are struggling to get to a higher income level, the no fluff strategies Katrina shares in this book make it a must-read primer." – Rebecca Ishibashi, Virtual Assistant

"Jumpstart Your New Business delivers... in a big way. I'm impressed with not only the examples but action-based tactics she explains in the book. After reading it, I still find myself referring back to the ideas and information as reference material." – Jen Crowe

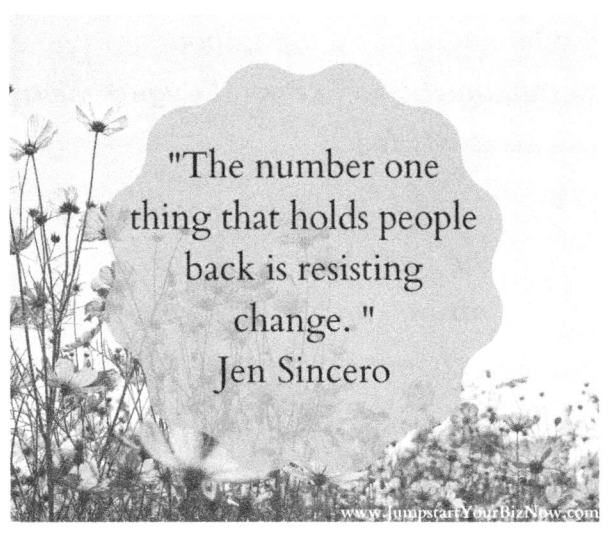

Jumpstart Your New Business Now!

The Entrepreneur's Guide to Starting & Growing a Profitable Business Doing What You Love!

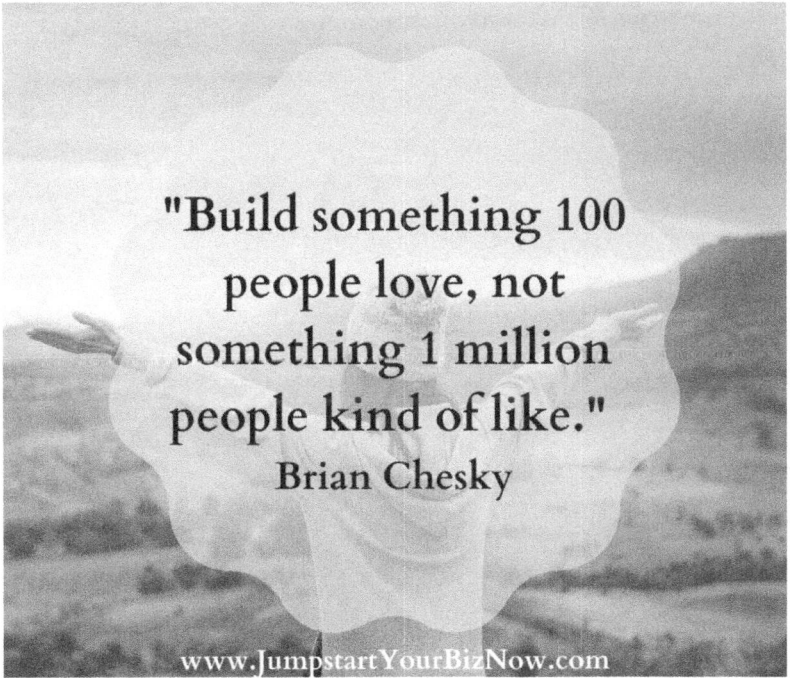

"Build something 100 people love, not something 1 million people kind of like."
Brian Chesky

www.JumpstartYourBizNow.com

Table of Contents

Introduction 1

Chapter 1: Big Goals 7

Chapter 2: Lifestyle Vision 11

Chapter 3: Reality Check 17

Chapter 4: Motivation Killers 29

Chapter 5: Passion & Purpose 35

Chapter 6: Starting Point 41

Chapter 7: Clearing Space 59

Chapter 8: Business Models 69

Chapter 9: Time to Sell 119

Chapter 10: Online Set-Up 137

Chapter 11: Relationship Marketing 159

Chapter 12: Team Building 173

Chapter 13: Advanced Strategies 181

Chapter 14: What's Next? 191

About the Author 195

"THE DIFFERENCE BETWEEN A SUCCESSFUL PERSON AND OTHERS IS NOT A LACK OF STRENGTH, NOT A LACK OF KNOWLEDGE, BUT RATHER IN A LACK OF WILL." — VINCE LOMBARDI

Introduction

Yes! You can do this... with this book and my help.

I had help to jumpstart my business with my very first mentor back in 2006 and you can too.

And I wish all it cost me was a $20 book!

I invested heavily for her expertise, even living month-to-month at the time. I had no idea how I was going to be able to cover her payments.

I knew it was going to work though. Somehow, I had unwavering faith that it would all work out in the end. And it did but let me tell you how it happened because you might be in a similar stage as I was.

Back then, I was a little over three years into my business, recently divorced and I'd grown my business to a high five-figure income, but it wasn't enough...not by a long shot.

I was working like a dog for that money though, on average about 60-70 hours a week. That was about the same number of hours as some of my jobs but at least there I had health benefits and vacation.

I had a new home that I'd purchased on my own and this was the first time I'd been technically in a "commission only" position.

You see, when I was in advertising sales for the local newspaper prior to starting my business, I had a base salary plus commission. And since I was pretty darn good at sales, I always earned a nice sized commission check every month. But a couple times I was almost swooned away by the radio advertising people except I always turned them down because, well, it was "commission only".

That scared me to death! What if I didn't perform one month?

Yet, somehow, having my own business was entirely different.

Not really... but it felt different to me.

So, back to my first mentor...

She literally helped me jumpstart my business in 90 days! I took massive action, changed everything and I worked really, really hard to make it happen. So, I know it's totally possible for you too.

I've worked with thousands of entrepreneurs since then and many have done the exact same thing.

Introduction

- Are you ready to move quickly to get to your goals faster? If so... this book will help you.

- Are you ready to finally have that dream business that you're passionate about? No more job or life you hate or that brings you down.

- Are you ready to show those in your life that YOU CAN DO THIS? You deserve to create the life of your dreams with a thriving business that brings in consistent profits every month, so you don't have to stress anymore about money.

Even if you already have a mentor, coach or mastermind group to help you in your business, *Jumpstart Your New Business Now* will absolutely show you how to transform your business into one you no longer have to stress about.

It will bring up things that you are not doing yet and that you'll want to be doing soon, especially if your goal is to build a smooth-running, moneymaking machine of a business.

A consistent revenue generating business doing what you love and giving you the life you want. That is my goal for you.

For some of you... you may be at the beginning stages of your entrepreneurial journey and a lot of what I share in this book will be new to you.

I say, "GREAT NEWS!" to that because it will literally shave off years of time and torture from your life to know this all sooner than later.

For others of you, you're reading this because you love to read about business, marketing, even self-help and if you learn just ONE thing you can implement or do differently to grow your business, it will have been worth your time.

And for the majority of you (I suspect), you're desperate for the REAL SCOOP on what it takes to build a consistent, successful, moneymaking business!

Either you've tried a bunch of things already or hired mentors, attended workshops, bought trainings and none of it has really gotten you to where you want to go. Or you've attained a certain level of success from it all but you know there's more that you're missing to get you to your "Next Level". Or you simply need someone to hold you accountable. I would LOVE to do that!!

Jumpstart Your New Business Now is for all of you.

Introduction

The strategies and training within this book were taken from my Jumpstart Your Business in 90 Days Home Study System (online course) that I used to sell for $1,997 on my website, and before that I taught it live for 3 years for $3,997.

I decided to transcribe and rewrite much of my curriculum into an easy-to-read book because I want to make this information more accessible to the masses. Then of course I've added to it and updated it for today's marketplace. Which is why this is now the 2nd edition!

It's very important to me that every entrepreneur or small business owner have the resources you need to transform your life by designing the business of your dreams.

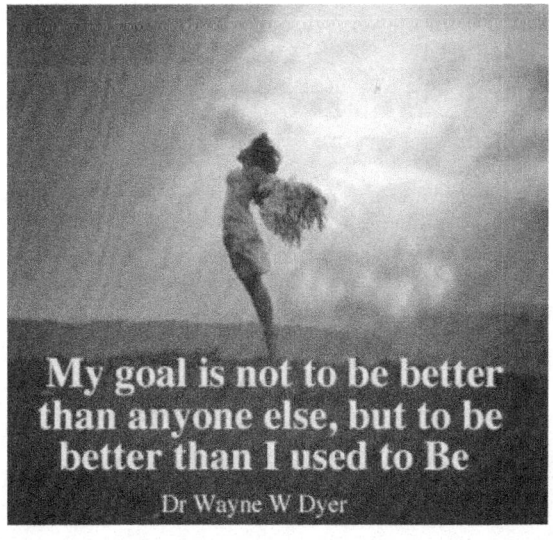

Chapter 1

Big Goals

"Whatever your money goal is, double or triple it! You're thinking way too small."
~ Katrina Sawa

Do you have…

- Big goals?
- Small goals?
- Mediocre goals?
- Goals that make your hair stand up?
- Goals that you're confident about?
- Goals that are so out there that you have NO idea how you'll accomplish them?

Fabulous! No matter what your answer is, that's fabulous, you know why?

Because you have goals!!

Yep, most entrepreneurs don't have goals. At least not clearly defined money and lifestyle goals that I talk about. So, you're clearly one step ahead.

And if you just picked one of those above but you really don't have any yet... that's ok, read closely though.

I want to encourage you to THINK BIGGER!

Set higher goals for yourself, your revenues and for what you REALLY want in your life as a whole.

I see way too many people settle and life is just too short to do that.

This book isn't really about goal setting at all, I'm assuming you have some already. I just want you to consider thinking bigger.

One reason why entrepreneurs don't make higher goals for themselves is; they tell me, "I don't want to work that hard". Which typically means that they equate making a lot of money with working harder or longer hours... that's simply not true. It can be, but it doesn't have to be.

One of my other mentors early on told me to think bigger too. He was referring to wanting millions of dollars in my business. "Why aren't you thinking in the millions?" he'd ask.

Big Goals

So, I drank the cool aid and set a 5-million-dollar goal.

Did that work out? No.

Don't do that if you haven't even gotten to $100,000 in revenues yet please.

But if you're thinking $50,000 in revenues, I'm suggesting, go for $75,000. If you're thinking $100,000, try $150,000.

And if you're not even thinking $50,000, why not? What's holding you back from thinking bigger?

Even if you've never made either amounts of money that I just referenced in a job before, it's possible to do that with almost any type of business.

You just may not know someone doing it or see people in your day-to-day, making such money.

I can tell you, that it is absolutely possible if you know what to do to accomplish that.

Then beyond the money goals, the lifestyle goals I think are much more important.

We're going to talk more about what you really want in life, your relationships and more throughout the book. Be open to thinking bigger and know that YOU DO DESERVE IT!

> **LIVE BIG!**
> Set a goal so big that if you achieved it, it would blow your mind.

Chapter 2

Lifestyle Vision

"Stop settling with a job that you hate or a relationship that's not serving you, life is too short."
*~ **Katrina Sawa***

Lifestyle goals help you outline HOW you want to live, HOW you want to spend your time, plus they help you realize and ensure you don't forget to include things and people that are really important to you.

For example, my lifestyle goals now are:

- Spend weekends with my family
- Get off work by 5 pm at the latest so I can cook dinner for or with my husband and family
- Enjoy my home, our yard, and entertain more
- Take care of my body and health so having time for exercise, eating healthy, relaxation and enough sleep

- Not traveling too much each year to speak or network

- Doing more online calls with clients and group calls with prospects

- Hosting my own live retreats and events locally more often to encourage and train clients

- Make an effort to see family and friends more often as well as grow my local friend pool

- Having my team take care of everything that I don't enjoy doing or do well

- Start investing in real estate so my money can make money and build more lifetime wealth

And what kind of money goal do I need to be able to have that?

Well, it's a lot more than I generate today as I write this. Although, you'd think what I do earn would be enough. It's not.

There's always a "next level" to get to when you're an entrepreneur, especially one that thinks bigger like me.

Plus, we have a 14-year-old, my stepdaughter Riley, who will probably need help in college, or for a wedding.

Lifestyle Vision

And who knows if I may have to help out my mom in her later years? Right now, she's managing well with her own finances and so are Jason's parents, but you never know!

What if we live until we're 95? Yikes, that sounds scary, but it could happen, and you have to be able to afford those later years which can get expensive if you do end up needing more medical assistance.

You just never know what you'll need 10, 20 or 30 years from now. The world could change dramatically.

What IF, you haven't set yourself up enough to live the life you want?

Doing all of what I mentioned and planning for your future too really does take a lot more money than you may think.

NOW is the time to generate as much revenue and income as humanly possible. Please stop thinking too small.

What do you want your lifestyle to look like in the next 3, 5, 10 or even 20 years? I want you to jot down 5 to 10 important deal breakers for you such as:

> *I will not be happy unless I am living in Florida on the beach, with my beach house and working*

from my laptop for five hours a week and that's all I want to be doing in 10 years.

Be very, very, very specific. What do you want your lifestyle to look like? It can involve work, it can involve your personal life, your love life, your kids, traveling... anything you want.

One thing I know is when you become aware of something you really want, it's more on top of mind with you.

Let me give you an example of what NOT to ask for though okay?

I had a client a few years ago who caught herself putting out the wrong request to the Universe which actually limited her income.

She kept telling herself and putting it out there that she wanted to make $5,000 in her business. She even put it on her vision board – the number $5,000.

Here's the distinction though, what she meant was $5,000 per month. That's what she wanted to make in her business, but she didn't specify the "per month" part on her vision board.

She looked at that vision board every single day and guess what she made that year?

Lifestyle Vision

Yes, you guessed it. $5,000 total. That was it. That was before working with me of course!

So, get specific and clear.

Now that I've asked you this question, you're going to be more aware of the things you really want. I believe you can have almost anything that you want, we just have to set a plan in place to make it happen. But most people don't know WHAT needs to go into that plan.

I also believe that your income is limitless when you run your own business. You can always make more money. You have to have the confidence that this can happen though. Do you?

RESOURCE:

- Need help to realize just how much money you could need to make to actually run a consistently profitable business? Go download my Need Number Worksheet online at www.JumpstartYourBizNow.com/neednumber. It will help you think of things you'll need to invest in or pay for each month that you may not be thinking of (hence you could need a bigger money goal).

Jumpstart Your New Business Now!

Chapter 3

Reality Check

"Running a smooth-running, consistent moneymaking business does take a bit of work to set up the right way from the start, but it's soooo worth it in the long run."
~ Katrina Sawa

Like I mentioned in the last couple chapters, the reality check is that we will need a LOT of money to live the life we want for the rest of our lives!

And if you are an entrepreneur then it's all up to you.

There's no time to wait. You never know what life is going to throw at you.

My husband, Jason, went through throat cancer the year we got engaged. He was diagnosed just 3 weeks after he proposed, at age 45! We had to postpone our wedding a year while he did treatments. It was horrible. I had to care for him a lot that year and work less than expected. It was unexpected and set us back financially too. Thankfully he survived and is still around today!

I had to undergo two total hip replacements the year before that, when I was 42 and 43. Granted, because I did them both in one year, it was basically a buy one get one free deal due to my insurance minimums, but that financial outlay and the fact that I had to take off weeks to recover twice that year, resulted in bankruptcy for me.

I had to go take care of my mom a few years in a row, traveling out of state to her, when she would fall and hurt herself – that happened three times until we finally moved her here!

And as horrible as those things were, we have friends who have been through way worse! Some loss of homes in a devastating fire. Others death of a spouse or child unexpectedly. How long does it take to overcome the sadness and grief in those types of situations? A long time.

All of those situations put a strain on and limited my time to work in or on the business. And anyone facing anything like these situations usually aren't prepared for them. I call this the "What If".

Reality Check

If I hadn't had some of the systems, team and automated marketing and follow up that I had in place I would have lost a lot of income.

Some business owners I know have things happen like that and don't have systems in place or a team to support them and when life hits, they are completely devastated. The loss of income sets them into foreclosure, bankruptcy or even going back to get a JOB.

I want to help you avoid this by sharing exactly how to set up, run and grow a business that will bring in consistent revenue for you for a long, long time so that you can design and enjoy your happiest life ever!

It's so important for small business owners and entrepreneurs to really learn how to grow a successful moncy-making business around what you're most passionate about. So many of us dive into our own business, and we don't focus on the big picture plan or the nitty gritty marketing. We often have no idea how it all flows together.

We just kind of dive in...

This is what I want to sell, do you want to buy it?

This is what I have to offer, do you want to take advantage of it?

Or do you want to get into my program?

You do this often without having a real good road map of what you plan to do, how you're going to launch your business and how much marketing you actually need to do in order to reach the money goal that you want to reach.

Times have changed since the Pandemic, and you have to know how to change with it.

When I first started my business, I went to the Small Business Association and the nonprofit business resource center. The people from SCORE (previously known as the Service Corps of Retired Executives) told me I had to do a business plan. So, I took a little course on it, and I developed this 28-page beautiful business plan with projections and forecasting and budgeting and everything.

Within a week or so it went into a drawer, and I never looked at it again.

This book is not about doing that. It's about developing and keeping your big picture vision of where you really want to be in 3, 5, 10, 20 years, on the top of your mind at all times--every week, almost every day if you can.

Reality Check

And guess what? Those goals and lifestyle desires will change for you over the years too! You have to be open to the evolution of you and your business.

It's ok to change your mind on what you want to do along the way.

It's ok to have different ideas of how you want your life to be.

It's also ok if you end up desiring one thing and your significant another. That's what happened to me and my first husband. We grew apart after I started my own business. I wanted more and he wanted things to remain the same.

I have a vision board for example that I keep right by my computer, near my desk that I look at every day. I have my top 7 to 10 goals on it, the big annual goals. I put pictures of things I want (or have wanted in past years) such as a new house, yard, car, love life, speaking, etc. And I even had Oprah's picture on it for a while because I wanted to be on her show.

All of the things I wanted, came to fruition in one way or another too because they were on top of mind with me at all times.

Vision boards (or vision videos too these days) can help to remind you every day of WHY you need to stay focused. Do you have one? Do you update it annually if so?

You also have to know where you are, and where you're starting out. Really look at your big picture vision and then what areas of your life or business need restructuring in order to free up some of your time.

The first thing you want to do as you read this is figure out how to free up some of your time so we can show you where to focus.

Most likely you're not doing the right activities every day or week to get you to the goals you want to achieve. You're probably wasting your time and money in some of the wrong places.

You're already too busy though, am I right?

If you have a full-time job right now and you're trying to start a business, you're too busy.

If you have a business already running, you're probably too busy doing the things you think you need to do (or that you've been told by others to do). In this book we want to dive into your time and mindset management, your purpose and your overall vision for monetizing your passions.

Reality Check

You're going to find out how to manage your time better, focusing on the right activities, instead of just adding more onto your plate. We want you to be more efficient on what you are doing and how to get the right things done faster.

We're going to focus on the big picture planning including developing your mindset and fine tuning your motivation. We're going to address some of the systems that are needed to get you to the next level. Then we're going learn how to have fun doing what you love, while designing the business around the lifestyle you want live rather than fitting your life in around your business.

We will take you from A to Z in starting, growing, marketing and really maximizing your business online, offline, locally, and globally.

It doesn't matter what you sell, this will work for any business. There may be a couple things here and there that might not fit with you and that's fine but overall, it's going to be a huge awaking, also a training, and education.

Throughout this book as well, there may be a few things I recommend or suggest but if they are not a good fit for everyone, I will mention that.

One of my biggest pet peeves with gurus and mentors out there is that they recommend something like a specific technology to "everyone" without indicating that it may not be good for those with x, y or z businesses.

I see entrepreneurs all the time get caught up in "bright shiny objects" or with strategies that are NOT good for you, or at least not yet. As much as I can in this book, I will share the "order of importance" of how you want to consider doing things.

You can read this book quickly or take your time and implement along the way. The concepts in this book are taken from my Jumpstart Your Business in 90 Days Home Study System like I said. So, by reading it, you could learn what to do to jumpstart your business and actually do it in 90 days but it's likely that it could take you longer than that to implement all the strategies in this book. Most of my coaching clients work with me for 3 to 7 years in fact. I know that may seem like a long time to be building your business but I'm in year 21 of my business now and I'm still learning, growing and investing in mentors myself. There is *always* a next level to achieve, and your dreams and desires will change along the way.

Reality Check

Remember I transformed my business in 90 days way back when, but I did it with a mentor holding me accountable and telling me what to do and not do.

You may also wish to get some coaching once you dive into these strategies more as well as a "next step".

At the end of the 90-days or however long it takes you hopefully you will implement all or many of the strategies in this book. Plus, as I write this, I do plan to write a series of books about jumpstarting all areas of your business and life so you can look out for those too.

By the time you've finished this book you also will have hopefully increased your rates. (If you don't or still can't, please pick up a copy of my other book, *Love Yourself Successful!*)

Hopefully soon after you read this and implement the strategies I teach; you will have gotten clients at the new rates, and you will have a really functional website that's bringing you new leads each month.

You will know exactly which marketing strategies to do and spend time on every week when you're done, how to do them, how to accomplish them, and how to maximize every opportunity available to you. (Keep in mind too however that with the social media marketing and online strategies, those change often so you need to reach out, continue learning more about those and possibly even attend my events or Online Group Programs!)

There are new marketing and business strategies that come into play each year, so you still want to continue learning, studying and having mentors. Don't ever stop learning or you may stop growing.

While reading this book, I would imagine you'll see more opportunities right in front of your face that you're not even seeing now because you're too busy or bogged down with some of the details that you shouldn't be.
We're going to walk you through my 10-step jumpstart your business in 90-days system. My hope is, that along the way, you're going to develop your system or signature process if you don't already have one. We'll show you how to repurpose it, monetize it, and sell it. You'll get clarity around what it is you're selling, who it's for, why and how to best monetize this business.

Now, for those of you who sell products where you can't raise your rates or charge what you want, or even create a system like I just mentioned... I want you to think for a moment and ask yourself, "why not"? What if there was another type of business model that you could add to what you're doing today that could bring you a lot more income each year? What if? It could be complimentary to what you're doing now. You may find that what you're doing now won't financially get you to where you ultimately want to be, and you might have to release it and move on to something else. I don't know but be open to everything.

I continue to learn more each month myself so make sure you get on my email list and follow my emails, my videos on YouTube, Facebook posts and even consider attending a live training or two for more up to date business and marketing strategies.

Let's get to work, shall we?

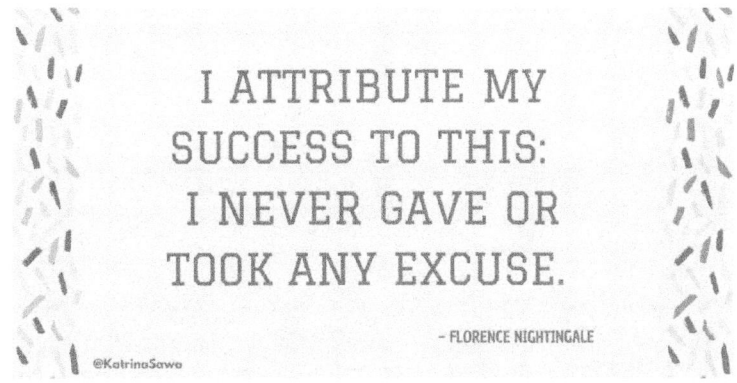

Chapter 4

Motivation Killers

"Get rid of the toxic people in your life that don't get you or who aren't supportive, they are holding you back."
~ Katrina Sawa

So, what motivates you? Entrepreneurs don't reach your goals sometimes because you just don't want it enough.

Are you motivated by money?

- Time Off?
- Vacation?
- Freedom?
- Family?
- Rewards?
- Recognition?

It's not always money that motivates people which, if this is you, it means you may not be interested in focusing a lot of your time on revenue generating activities. Not good!

I had one client a few years ago who had two full-time businesses that were each making over a $100,000 a year but she had three kids and she never saw them. She had a husband too and a not so happy marriage.

For her, making more money wasn't the motivator, it was systematizing, automating and delegating in her business to free up some of her time so she could spend it more with her kids and her family.

I had another client who was a fitness trainer in New York City. She ran all over town doing private sessions with clients and teaching classes at gyms.

She was so busy and hardly ever home and even for NYC not making the best of money either.

The problem was that what her big vision and dream had always been to get married and have children.

First of all, she was almost too busy to find a man that she would want to marry let alone have time to date.

Secondly, she had been told that she wasn't going to be able to have children by doctors.

Motivation Killers

But all that changed once she started changing up her business and business models.

When I got my hands on her and her business, she really allowed herself to think differently about how she could make money doing what she loved.

She opened her mind to new ideas including training people online over video on how to do the exercises they needed to do to lose weight or achieve their goals.

Once she created her Fit and Healthy Tribe online doors started opening for her all over the place. She also met a man and fell in love.

They got married, she moved out of the city and really embraced her new online business models. But best of all is that God blessed her with two happy, healthy boys.

Now, she has the life of her dreams which honestly doesn't have anything to do with making a million dollars. But to her it's worth the same.

So, you have to really think about what motivates you--if it's not money then how can you change your thinking about that?

Remember... What If? You need to have money in case something happens to you or a loved one especially so that you don't get taken off course.

I've had other clients who have huge missions in life, and they want to change the world. If this is you, you might focus the majority of your time on serving and giving to others not realizing however that to see your dream and mission come true, it will take a lot of funding!

I believe no matter what your initial motivator is, you still have to figure out how to get motivated by money. Take a couple minutes and jot a few things down that come to mind on what motivates you.

What will make me get motivated about making more money? (Jot down some thoughts right here!)

_____
_____
_____
_____
_____
_____
_____

Motivation Killers

Another motivation killer are all the negative thoughts and stuff you're thinking that would prevent you from getting what you want or making your goals. I call that your "head trash".

What do you feel is stopping you from doing this, or thinking you can't have this as a business, or thinking you can't make money at this?

What is getting in your way? What head trash is going on in your mind that's getting in the way of you living that type of lifestyle?

Are you believing you won't have it or stalling you from taking action towards building the kind of business that will create the kind of lifestyle you want?

Write it all down, be honest with yourself. What are you also tolerating in your life that maybe you feel like you can't control?

Being aware of these things is the first step to getting through it, getting over it or letting it go.

Jumpstart Your New Business Now!

What are your top three limiting beliefs around living this type of lifestyle or having this type of business?

1. _____

2. _____

3. _____

Chapter 5

Passion & Purpose

"It's time to finally take charge of your life and design the business and life of your dreams!"
~ Katrina Sawa

Now... what are you really passionate about?

Are you doing a business that you're really passionate about? If so, great, you can skip ahead to the next chapter now.

If you're not doing a business that you're 100% passionate about yet or you're still in the beginning stages of thinking what you want to do for a business then keep reading...

The reason I talk about passion and purpose is because I don't see a lot of highly successful and profitable business owners who are not passionate about what they're doing.

Typically those who aren't passionate about what they do don't last that long in business. They don't make as much money, they switch companies or businesses often or all of the above!

I do believe you can build a successful moneymaking business around almost anything you're passionate about. You just may not know HOW.

Write a couple things down that you're really passionate about such as:

- Helping others in general (or be specific like: to lose weight, stress less, get organized, eat healthier, be more confident, etc.)

- Solving problems of some sort (this is how I see what I do, I help solve the problem of not making money doing what you love and how to grow your business with more ease and systems for freedom)

- Supporting people in some way (such as a bookkeeper, housekeeper, accountant, personal assistant)

- Doing a specific craft (such as being a personal chef, massage therapist, event planner, speaker, etc.)

Passion & Purpose

What we want to find out right now is if you're doing or planning to do something that you're meant to do or not.

By writing this down, it's possible that you realize, holy crap, I'm in the wrong business!

If you have a passion for helping people ease their pain through massage therapy, and you're doing mortgage loans, that's not serving you.

So, think about what you're doing, what you're an expert in and what you're really passionate about right now and pick whatever sounds good for you to start a business doing today. (Hint: You can always change your mind and change your business later! Yes, you can!!)

If you need to make money right away, then pick something that you're already good at doing or know how to do first because you'll have more immediate confidence in that thing, and it will be easier for you to ask for the business.

For example, if you're leaving a job where you do bookkeeping for a company right now, and what you really want to do is health coaching, then perhaps start off taking bookkeeping side jobs to pay the bills while learning more about how to become a health coach, get certified, develop your programs, get a few clients under your belt, etc.

You can always change or evolve your business later, even though it may not be the exact thing you want to be doing ultimately 5, or 10 years from now.

Another example is that you've been home raising your kids for 14 years and now you're ready to get back into the workplace. One of your kids has autism and you have a passion for developing a local center for parents and their autistic kids to help them cope with the day-to-day, take classes, offer childcare, etc. You don't currently have $250,000 to buy or lease commercial property or do a build out for that center just yet. You need to produce some funding so you can turn your dream into a reality.

So, you need to develop either a business, or a non-profit or some sort of way to generate those funds (and a really profitable business plan) to create this. What do you know how to do now? What can bring in bigger dollars, not just selling a supplement type of product from a network marketing company for example. Not that doing network marketing companies are bad to do, but most who do them, don't bring in more than a couple thousand dollars a month unfortunately.

In this example, you'd want to get guidance from someone like me who can give you multiple options on what kind of business you could do now to raise the capital. It might not be exactly what you ultimately want to do, but for a couple years, it could be a means to the bigger financial goal and desires. Understand?

Your business will evolve, you have to trust me when I say this. What you're building today will not be what you end up with in three years, maybe even next year!

Be open to the evolution of your business, your life and your mindset along the way.

17 HARD THINGS YOU HAVE TO DO TO BE A GREAT LEADER

You have to make the call you're **afraid** to make.
You have to **get up earlier** than you want to.
You have to give more than you get in return right away.
You have to care more about others than they care about you.
You have to feel unsure and insecure when playing it safe seems smarter.
You have to lead when **no one else is following** you yet.
You have to invest in yourself even though no one else is.
You have to grind out the details when it's easier to shrug them off.
You have to deliver results when making excuses is an option.
You have to search for your own explanations even when you're told to accept the "facts".
You have to make mistakes and **look like an idiot**.
You have to **try and fail and try again**.
You have to run **faster** even though you're out of breath.
You have to be kind to people who have been cruel to you.
You have to meet deadlines that are unreasonable and deliver results that are unparalleled.
You have to be accountable for your actions even when things go wrong.
You have to keep moving towards where you want to be no matter what's in front of you.

♥ LESLEYMYRICK.COM

Chapter 6

Starting Point

"Just Do It!"
~ **Nike** *(and* **Katrina Sawa** *on many occasion)*

What does your business look like today?

Where are you now?

Do you think you should be making more money than you are right now based on how long you've been in business?

Are you working too hard, too many hours?

Long hours are not necessarily an indication that you're doing well in business, sometimes it's an indication of the fact that you don't have the right systems, plan or structure in place.

I used to work into the wee hours of the night a long time ago but I don't do that anymore. I take weekends off now and most days don't work more than eight hours, some days far less.

Jumpstart Your New Business Now!

Very rarely do I get on the computer after 6:00 PM, and I hardly ever talk to anybody or do anything before 9 or 10 AM. Because that's the kind of life I designed for myself, so think about that.

What does your business look like today – where are you now? (Think about the following areas in your business and see where you are with each.)

- Are you making money yet? Enough?
- Are you working too hard?
- Do you know who your ideal target client is and what they really want or need?
- Does your product or service meet their needs?
- Do you have a good closing ratio?
- Are you asking for the sale enough?
- Are you charging enough?
- Do you have leveraged programs, products and services in place to offer or do you still only trade hour for dollar with clients?
- Do you have at least 5-10 different marketing strategies in place and running consistently?
- Do you have an effective, lead generating website?

Starting Point

- Are you focused weekly on list building and lead generation?

- Are you sending weekly emails to your subscribers or two emails a month at minimum so they don't forget about you?

- Do you have a team in place yet or at least one Virtual Assistant?

- Do you know where you ultimately want to take your business? How Big? How Much $$ do you want to make?

- Have you outlined specific goals you're working on achieving?

- Do you speak in front of groups to leverage your time?

- Do you set boundaries for your time and when you're available and not available?

- Do you time block your calendar so you can get more done?

- Do you have a mentor or two that you can speak to one-on-one for more specific and custom advice?

- Do you love what you're doing and how you're doing it?

I know this list could sound pretty overwhelming. I promise you'll be much clearer and more focused about all of this stuff before you get to this end of this book.

If you've already got all this in place, no worries, there's more to do and implement! If not, no worries, I will walk you through all of this, I promise.

Target Market

Are you super clear on who your ideal target is and what they really want or need?

You don't have to have a "niche" necessarily by the way. I realize many people will tell you that you do, or in fact that it's critical!

I look at niches a little differently.

You do need to have an idea of the kind of people you want to work with or the kinds of problems that you want to solve.

Sometimes the niche is that type of problem but many different types of people. Other times the niche is how you work with people.

For example, maybe you only want to work virtually, then your niche is someone whose problems you solve doing that online.

Starting Point

Think about your ideal target market. What are their probable demographics as well as possible Psychographics.

Demographics are basic characteristics like:

- Marital status
- Education
- Income level
- Age
- Race

Psychographics are lifestyle characteristics such as:

- Prefer quality over discounts
- Online shoppers
- Personality traits
- Values
- Interests like read magazines

You want to think about the 75 to 80 percent of the people that you work with, or that you could see yourself working with, which of these can you determine as a common quality?

Now that's pretty broad I get it, but the point is that I don't recommend you focus on figuring out your "niche" too early on in your business or doing that will slow you down.

Your niche ultimately works itself out over time. You can't and shouldn't force it if you aren't sure what it is in the beginning.

My "niche" for example, is not a particular type of business like a coach, or a business in a certain stage like a startup. My niche is a business whose owner is highly motivated to live the life of their dreams and know they need to make a LOT of money doing it to enjoy that lifestyle. They also know they need guidance on things they aren't experts in to learn what they need to do to get there. That's my niche.

Marketing Messages

Even if you've been in business for 10, 15, 20 years sometimes you still are not clear with your marketing message, or you evolve and so does your niche or focus. This could mean that what you are doing in your marketing is no longer proving to be effective.

You need to make it super clear and not confusing at all as to what it is you do and how you can help your clients and customers.

You want to find out the Hot Buttons of your ideal target market and then turn those into Headlines,

Offers, Product Names, Webinar Titles, Article Titles, eBook Titles, Books, Speeches, and more.

EXERCISE: Go talk to a few of your current customers or ideal prospects.

Ask them what the reasons are that they came to work with you or why they initially bought. Write down EXACTLY what they say and turn those words around into headlines and marketing copy.

If they say a statement like, "I want to lose weight" your headline would read:

Do you want to lose weight?

Or if they say, "I'm tired of buying a bunch of lotions and potions; I want a real anti-aging solution." Then you turn those words around into a headline that reads:

Tired of buying a bunch of lotions and potions? Want a REAL Anti-Aging Solution that Works?

Just take their phrase and turn it around to a question and there is a really viable headline.

Just don't change *their words* to *your words,* even if they aren't as sophisticated.

Using the first response for example, don't change the headline to read:

Shed some pounds this summer!

Because that's not what they're saying they want!

In the beginning when you're trying to set up these basics there is too much to do. You don't have time to dwell on what to write or say on your marketing materials and website, just go with what sounds good today and change it later if you have to.

In fact, as I'm updating this book in 2023, ChatGPT and other AI tools are abundant. People are using these tools for brainstorming, keyword research, content outlining and development. It's not a bad thing to use AI copywriting tools for these reasons, I would just say to customize it afterwards a bit to fit you, your voice and your ideal clients.

I did a short 10-minute speech around Using AI in Your Marketing and it's on my YouTube if you go to my channel and search for AI.

What Are You Selling?

More important than almost anything, is what you're selling. If you aren't totally clear and confident about what you're offering, selling and how you work with clients then it will be harder to make a sale.

Starting Point

If you don't have products and services yet, then figure out what the needs are of that ideal prospect and then design your product or service around their needs. Make sure you're designing something that you actually want to design and provide as well as are passionate about.

And make sure you have a couple different types of business models too to create different price points and or leveraged income streams.

What do I consider a business model?

There is a whole chapter devoted to this topic because it's so important to choose your models wisely.

Next... Are you charging enough?

Unless you've been working with me for a while you're probably not.

That's one of the first things I do is I make people raise their rates. So look forward to getting a raise while reading this book. Don't worry we'll help you increase your confidence so you know you deserve it before you do it.

Closing Ratio

Do you have a good closing ratio?

If you're not closing at least 25% of the people, you actually have a real sales conversation with then you might want to work on your sales processes and language.

Most people who don't close or enroll at least 25-50% of the prospects they speak to often don't have the right WORDS to do so, or they aren't able to effectively "dance with the person's concerns" (manage objections).

It could be any of the following things that are slowing you down from making more sales:

- The sales talk you're using (the actual words)
- You talk more than you listen, and you aren't hearing people and their problems clearly
- You don't ask enough questions
- You get pressured to tell them how much too early on in the conversation
- You're not asking for the sale or wait too long to do so
- You're not showing enough value
- You're emailing proposals instead of scheduling follow up calls to review them

Starting Point

- You're talking about your program, product or services too soon in the conversation or too much

- You aren't skilled enough to handle all the objections well

- You don't believe your products or services are worth what you're charging (this is why I always say charge as much as you can say without stuttering – when you stutter over price, you lose the sale)

One thing I'm really good at is giving clients the "words" to say in conversations like these. I talk through scenarios with clients before and after your calls and presentations.

Are you asking for the sale enough? I had one client admit that she doesn't ask for the sale. She gets really nervous when it comes to asking for the sale and so she just doesn't do it.

That's not helpful though, right? The right people may lean in and ask YOU how to work with you or buy, but that's a rarity.

We need to help you get past these fears and resistance if any of this is resonating with you.

We also want you to charge more for what you're offering... but you do have to be confident in your rates and prices so do your best and keep raising them as your confidence raises!

If you know sales is an area you're not strong in, this is something you want to fix and work on sooner than later. Your marketing and sales strategies and processes are the lifeblood of your business!

If you'd like to have a coaching session with me now or while you're going through this book to go through the sales conversation or anything at all, just go to the book resources page on my site and sign up.

I developed a private page just for those of you who have this book with opportunities for discounted calls with me as well as many other free and low-priced resources, videos, trainings, checklists and more. You can find all of this online at www.JumpstartYourBizNow.com/JumpstartBookResources.

I love sales and selling! I know, that's weird. But I've literally been doing sales since my first job as an ice cream scooper at Thrifty's, a drug store in my town back in 1986. Yes, I realize that dates me!

Starting Point

But it was easy to sell customers up from one scoop of ice cream to two or three! Right? You could do that. You believe in people getting what they want, like more ice cream.

You have to believe in what you're offering wholeheartedly though.

My second job was working in a clothing store in the mall. I worked there because I enjoyed wearing the popular styles and my parents couldn't always afford to buy me all the clothes I wanted. I became good at selling customers there into buying a shirt to go with their pants or jewelry with their outfit.

Upsells were fun! It was a challenge to see just how much I could get someone to buy.

I did that for a friends' mom's florist during college too over Valentine's Day week. Selling the men up from buying only a dozen roses to a dozen roses, stuffed bear, chocolates and balloons!

You might be thinking "that's not good", but I would bet that those men got *exactly* what they wanted after splurging on their woman like they did! Plus, they wouldn't have done it if they couldn't.

You can't prejudge your prospects either. You don't know what they can afford and what they can't. You can't make decisions for them either!

Every once in a while, I have a client who says, "her prospects can't afford her services if she charges more" and she believes this to her core. But, often times, it's HER insecurities around being able to afford things that she's projecting on her prospects. Don't do that.

That's why you have to work on your own limiting beliefs along with improving your own closing and selling techniques.

It's your job to make the right offers to the right people for the right reasons. How much you charge for those offers though should solely depend on what YOU feel valued for, not just on what you believe people can afford. You just want to go find people who CAN afford what you want to sell! That means changing up your marketing strategy perhaps. Pay attention to this.

Starting Point

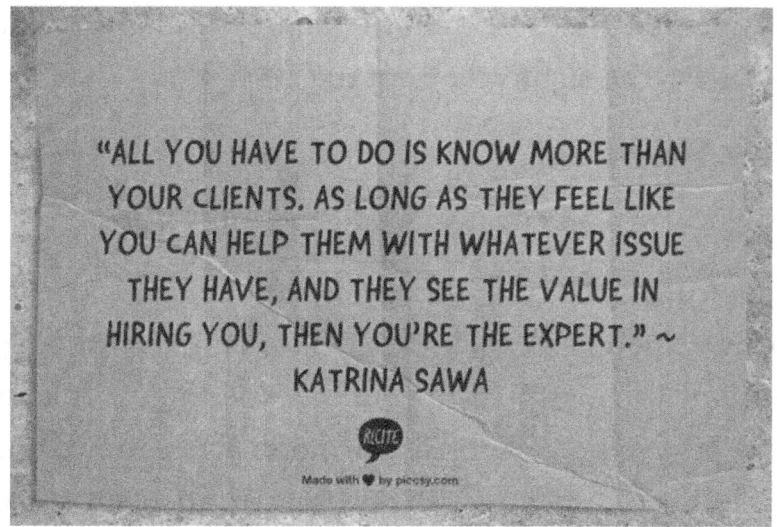

Marketing

Do you have at least 5-10 different marketing strategies in place and running consistently?

One of the ways I teach about marketing is that there are three different types of marketing:

1. New Business Marketing

2. Database Marketing

3. Referral Source Marketing

There are various strategies under each category that you want to focus on, and you might want to schedule in 2-10 hours a week to do marketing activities. I'll get more into the marketing soon, but first I have a few more things to share about setting up the business the right way from the start.

Your Website

Do you have an effective lead generating website?

That's one of the first things I look at with new clients because you can't really do a lot of online marketing without driving them to your website to get on your list, buy something or learn more. Even the offline leads need systems within your site to push them through the sales process.

Doing business these days without investing and focusing a lot on your online presence, purpose and business strategy is one of the biggest mistakes entrepreneurs can make. In fact, if you're not updating your website every couple years, you're most likely utilizing outdated technology, keywords, and functionality.

This is NOT an area that you want to do yourself either. I know web designers who hire other web designers to build their websites because they realize that doing our own marketing or website is not a good plan. You're too close to your business to be objective about what your prospects need to see and experience on your website.

Starting Point

You need to have some kind of opt in on your website. We're going to talk a lot about your website, this is where a lot of the automation happens when you can get leads coming in without you having to work at it. And that results in more freedom and time in your life.

Team

Do you have a team in place yet or at least one virtual assistant?

If not it's okay, but you're going to see how important it is to surround yourself with the people that can do things that you don't like to do, don't want to do, and don't know how to do. You want to find those that can do it much faster, more efficiently and better than you.

I'll show you exactly what to delegate so you don't just go hire a random assistant to do random tasks. You want to be very strategic with your team building, even if you just start with hiring someone for a couple hours a month.

FREE RESOURCE: Want to learn about how to hire a team or an assistant the right way from the

Jumpstart Your New Business Now!

start plus what to delegate? I have a comprehensive eBook and checklist for you for just $27 on my site at www.JumpstartYourTeam.com!

There is freedom in building boundaries around yourself and not apologizing for them.

b.oakman | *Survival Fences*

Chapter 7

Clearing Space

"You've got to say NO to some things to open up time in your schedule to do the moneymaking activities that need to get done."
~ Katrina Sawa

What do I mean by clearing space?

It's about your time management and how to manage your calendar.

I get that you're already too busy to add more of what I'm suggesting you do in this book, therefore, we have to figure out how you can clear some space first!

We need to identify areas where you can:

- Stop working so hard
- Maybe get rid of some of the activities you're currently doing
- Automate certain things
- Delegate some other things

- And/or systematize specific processes or things that you're doing so it frees up your time more

- Let go of specific obligations you may have that are no longer serving you to make room for more of what matters most these days

Take time over the next week to do the following exercise.

EXERCISE: Keep a pad of paper or journal handy by your desk or by your side for an entire week. Write down everything that you're doing every minute of every day.

Look back on that list a week later and see where you feel like you wasted time with something, something that could have been done by someone else or how often you weren't contributing to real sales and marketing activities.

An example of something you could automate to save time:

> When you get a new client and you have to manually send an email to them with an attachment of a questionnaire to have them fill out before your first call. That can be automated by creating a fill in form on your

Clearing Space

website that people fill out instead. On top of that, you get a copy of their answers and they get sent an automated email with their next steps. No manual labor needs to be involved therefore saving you a few minutes, maybe more. But how many of THOSE minutes would add up over the course of a year? And that's just ONE example.

An example of something you could delegate to save time:

When you come back from a live event or conference with 15-50 business cards and you want to follow up with them. But first those business cards need to be entered into your database or email marketing system. That is one of the easiest things that can be delegated.

Data entry is not a good use of your time. In fact most of the things you send for follow up, the emails, cards or direct mail, even social media connecting can be delegated. I just wouldn't recommend delegating the follow up phone calls unless you have an expert sales strategist on your team who knows how to convert prospects well or identify who would be best for scheduling a call with you.

Let's identify some areas where you could automate, delegate, or systematize processes.

EXERCISE:

- **List 10-12 tasks or things that you're doing now (personal or business) that you feel are NOT contributing to your money-making success?** Check that big list you made that week you kept track.

- **What are some of the tasks or things you WANT to be doing that you aren't?** (personal or business) For example, one thing I know I wanted to start doing this year was writing and sending out a printed newsletter in the mail. I knew in order to do this, I needed to get a couple things off my plate too but also I needed to hire someone to design me a template and then be able to update that template quarterly before sending.

Accomplishing New Tasks

Set yourself up for success now and make a commitment to yourself to prioritize your tasks and only put on your to do list those things that you can successfully accomplish during the time allotted.

Clearing Space

Writing a book for example, should not go on your to do list in one day. It's just too big of a project. You want to break down the many activities that are involved with writing a book and prioritize them.

Then take one or two of those activities every week perhaps and put them on your list such as:

- Write the outline for the book
- Write the introduction to the book
- Delegate the cover design of the book
- Write your back cover copy
- Write chapter 1, 2, 3, etc.

Those are action items in writing a book. And PS – if you are or want to write a book, remember I have a book publishing company too and can help guide you in the process. I have a couple free trainings about book publishing and book marketing on my site at www.JumpstartPublishing.net.

Another thing that can totally free up a lot of your time is to give up listening to free teleclasses, webinars and videos, perhaps even certain podcasts that share fluff type of advice and not real step-by-step strategy; especially while you're reading this book because it might confuse you.

I know many of you are saying "No!" right now to this advice. "But there is so much free information and training online, why would I stop listening to it all?"

Because the free advice you're hearing, I'll bet, is all over the board.

One day you hear that you need to know about Facebook marketing and so you go listen to a few people about Facebook. Maybe you change some things on your Facebook profile or page after that and maybe you don't.

Then the next day you hear someone saying that you need to host and run your own live events. You can't imagine doing that however so you disregard that advice. Or you love the idea and put an event on your calendar for the following month but you don't fill it very well at all because you didn't learn how to fill an event, just on how to host one. You focused more on the content you were going to deliver rather than who would care and how to get them to register.

I have example after example of situations like this where entrepreneurs come to me with a preconceived idea of what they think they need to do or what they have tried and not been successful at. Therefore they prejudge the advice I share due to supposedly having tried that strategy before and it not working.

Clearing Space

There's a method to my madness on things that I take you through and the sequence in which we implement. If you move them out of order or discover any bright shiny objects out there it could really slow you down and cost you money to boot!

Remember, the goal is to help you jumpstart your business to get more clients and make more money. Don't get distracted.

I do recommend you spend whatever time you need for self-care or family and you plot those things on your calendar first. For example, if you need to meditate in the morning and you need 30 minutes to do that, plot it on your calendar make sure it happens.

If you need two hours for when your kids get out of school to not work and spend time with them on homework and sharing, then plot it on your calendar and make sure it happens!

If you need a date night with your honey then plot it on your calendar and make sure you honor your relationship and make sure it happens.

If you need a girl's (or guys) night out on a Wednesday night then plot it on your calendar.

If you have other commitments such as church, volunteering or other networking groups, you can fill those in your calendar too.

It's very important to put yourself first, then your family, then your clients and then everyone else. Trust me, this is how you avoid burnout and even perhaps a divorce!

What are some ways you can change about your time management, habits?

Think about it.

Ready to set up your time management commitments?

In order for you to create the smooth-running, moneymaking business that brings you consistent revenue doing what you love, you want to spend a minimum number of hours a week working ON your business, not just IN it.

Clearing Space

I recommend putting on your calendar a minimum of 2-10 hours a week to plot out your marketing tasks, follow up, make website changes, reach out to prospects, think up new ideas, attend effective groups for networking, speaking, and more.

EXERCISE: Write out what you will commit yourself to on the following (fill in the blank):

- **I'm going to spend ____ hours working on my business every week and I've plotted the time on my calendar to make this happen.**

Keep in mind too that I developed a private page just for those of you who have this book with opportunities for discounted calls with me as well as many other free and low-priced resources, videos, trainings, checklists and more. You can find all of this online at www.JumpstartYourBizNow.com/JumpstartBookResources.

Jumpstart Your New Business Now!

Chapter 8

Business Models

"One business model does NOT fit all."
*~ **Katrina Sawa***

How do you work with clients? Some ways are more efficient and profitable than others. Do you have a variety of business models to fit a variety of price points or are you losing some people with limited options.

You want to first consider ways YOU would most like to work with your clients and customers as well as how THEY would most like to work with you or how they could consume your content and expertise.

Brainstorm the types of business models for example and then choose which ones you like most and do those.

- Will they want to talk with you directly one on one?

- Would they prefer learning and working in groups?

- Do they like phone sessions, classes or in-person events?

- Would they pay for a membership for ongoing learning or buy a product to do it themselves?

- How about teleclasses, video conferences and webinars?

- Will they only work with someone local or are they open to working with someone from anywhere?

Decide on which ones are right for you, which ones are right for your clients and which ones are right obviously for your ideal lifestyle.

Remember if you want your lifestyle to be working 20 hours a week from anywhere with a laptop then you might want to be careful adding certain in person business models into your plan.

Instead, for example, you might want to do more virtual events, webinars, group coaching programs online or one-on-one consulting or coaching.

Let's use bookkeeping as an example. A bookkeeper might charge $40 an hour to do someone's books.

Business Models

Then maybe they might do individual or business taxes for a flat fee of $600 annually but really there's nothing else in their business model; they just trade hour for dollar.

So what could a bookkeeper do to create additional business models and income streams?

One easy thing is if they aren't charging a retainer for their monthly work, they could do that. That would make it so they knew each month just how much money they would bring in. They could charge based on the client's average hours they typically spend or just develop a package that fits most. That could be set up as a recurring payment too through their shopping cart or accounting software so even less time spent on invoicing. My bookkeeper is also my CPA, but she charges me a flat $225/month for bookkeeping. Easy for me to budget, easy for her to count on. Get it?

They could also have other bookkeepers work underneath them and pay them $15-$20 per hour as contractors, making $20-$25 per hour themselves off the top in that $40/hour example.

In addition, the bookkeeper could run monthly trainings online or in person where they train businesses to do their own books or train other bookkeepers to start their own bookkeeping business. That would be a leveraged business model working one to many instead of one-on-one or hour for dollar where they could charge hundreds or even thousands of dollars per person each time they held it.

Another example is a Career Consultant. I've worked with a few Career Consultants before, usually coming into their own business from a long stent in corporate themselves. They want to help other executives from burnout or to increase their worth with their company and therefore get higher up the ladder and income bracket.

Most Career Consultants who come to be in this capacity however with this frame of mind, don't even see that they can perhaps charge $25,000 or more per year to work with them. To make $100,000 per year in this type of business, you could literally have 4 clients!

If this seems like a lot to you, it's not. Imagine someone is completely unhappy in their current position, not making enough money, ready for new responsibilities, challenges and a true rewarding career giving them a more fulfilling life. That person could see it worth $25,000 to invest in order to get

Business Models

the skills and new life they truly desire. Especially if they don't currently see how to get there themselves.

What people believe their need is worth is not your issue. If it's worth it to them, they will invest.

Sometimes it takes a few years to get the confidence to charge at such a level, it did for me too. But that doesn't mean you can't work towards that. You can take small baby steps getting there, increasing your rates $10/hour at a time if you want. Or you can take big leaps and double or triple your rates just like that, today because I'm telling you, there are plenty of people out there willing to pay whatever you want to charge, you just haven't found them yet.

And a third example is a person selling a product through a network marketing company, such as skin care, supplements, clothing, makeup and more. Those individuals are told by their parent company that they should give coaching to their downline to build more people under them as they make money from their downline's sales too.

They don't give a lot of guidance however in how to create additional income streams. One business model that could be good for this type of professional is a membership program.

Think about it, they have the perfect skin care or makeup products, but their customers don't often know which products will benefit what issues they may have such as reducing or hiding wrinkles, enhancing cheekbones, clearing up acne, etc.

Why not start a lower priced membership where your customers get access to advice and trainings from you and other professionals you might bring in to help them. Not everyone knows how to put on makeup, heck, my teenager was trying to figure it out herself when she started wearing makeup. I tried to help her out, but that was my way. She watched videos but boy were some of them crazy! Am I right? We need guidance in many areas of life and business.

Same thing goes for someone selling weight loss supplements, they could start a membership encouraging people to exercise or stay on track each week.

And someone selling a specific clothing line, why not have a membership where customers get access to special sales and discounts throughout the year or close out products, or special trunk sales in person. For a small fee, a second income stream that recurs each month or year, they can provide better service and a wow customer experience.

Business Models

Hopefully this is giving you some ideas on different business models or rate packages that you can use in your business.

It's important to think up some additional business models in order to add revenue streams, diversify what you're doing or leverage your time so you're not just trading hour for dollar. This is how those who make a lot of money do it.

You may also need or want to develop your new signature product or service. People like to buy solutions more than just a session.

For example, if you're a healer charging by the session right now, think about the overall transformation that you provide your clients over time. Then determine a package that you can create that helps them attain that transformation and charge for the total package as a "signature system or service" instead of a package of hours.

Then your signature talk or your free download from your website needs to be based on your process or system. If you have a seven step process then you have a seven point talk and you have a 7 step freebie.

It's very easy then to build the business faster and get rolling with clarity because you have a set process and everything flows together.

And I know we're moving kind of fast but there's a lot to do when starting up a business.

So, now, if you didn't have to worry about making money, how would you prefer to spend your time when working? Would you:

- Talk to people over the phone?
- Hold workshops or events in person or virtually?
- Speak at live events?
- Work behind the scenes creating tools and programs for others to consume?
- Have hands on products to sell?
- Do something else?

A lot of the people I work with are coaches or consultants of some kind who started off providing mostly one-on-one services.

I still do one-on-one myself because I love it. I also know that my ideal clients NEED it. It's the best thing for them to get where they want to go faster and without as many mistakes. So, I know it's what they need and am happy to do one-on-one with clients. I just charge accordingly for it. This should be one of your highest priced offerings. "Your genius is what you should charge the most for" is what I told a client once who was giving away advice, insight, and comforting words, to pretty much everyone she met.

I have a few clients who come to me and definitely know they do not want to do one-on-one coaching or services. They either have been burned out by it, had some not-so-nice clients or they've not been paid what they're worth which are reasons why they don't want to do it moving forward.

But those clients came in thinking that they had to charge a much lower fee for whatever reason. (Usually, basing their worth in limiting beliefs from childhood or their life.)

In fact, what if you charged $500 or $1,000 per hour, would one-on-one be worth it for you?

When I share that you can charge whatever you want for one-on-one, you can do it however you want, and you can accept whoever you want as a client, then it's a different story usually. People don't always realize it's up to you!

You might need to do some one-on-one of some sort during the first couple of years in your business. It's a lot easier to get clients this way rather than filling a group program when you don't have a lot of people on your email list.

Plus, working one-on-one with clients allows you to get insight on the process you take people through, their hot buttons and the feedback you need to grow and alter your programs.

Here are the main different types of business models that I share with most of my coaching clients. We choose the ones that fit their type of business, money goals, target market needs and lifestyle desires.

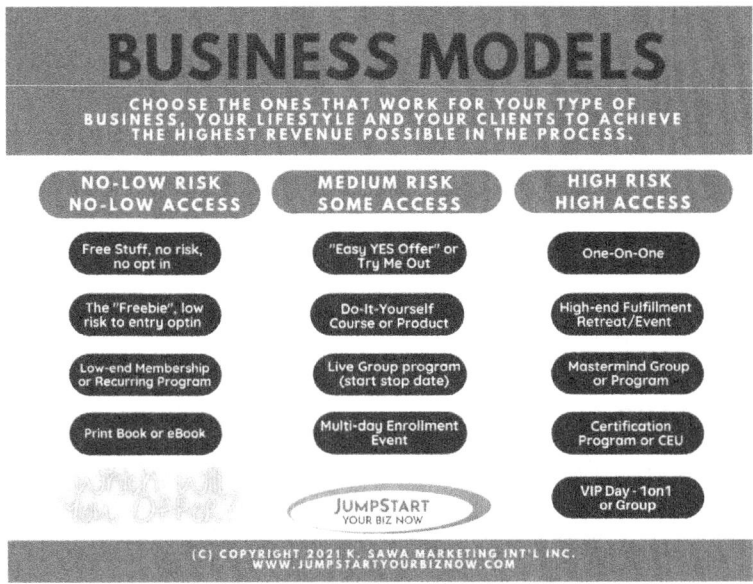

Business Models:

1. One-on-one coaching or consulting
2. Group training program
3. Online course
4. Hosting live events in person or virtual
5. Memberships (low or high priced)
6. Paid speaking
7. Retail business (Brick and mortar)
8. Online store (Physical products)
9. Affiliate marketing
10. Network marketing
11. Certification or licensing

Now let me dive into each one of these a little deeper in case you aren't aware of what they are or if they would work for you.

One-on-One

Working one-on-one with your clients is certainly a fine way to run your business. It's just hard to ever leverage what you're doing or scale it to make a lot more money. You can make as much as you can depending on how many hours you work times the price you charge per hour.

But what happens when you want to take a vacation? You don't get paid.

Or if you have to go take care of a loved one? You don't get paid unless you can manage it remotely.

Or if something happens to you or you have surgery and need recovery time with say, pain killers, and really can't work? You don't get paid.

I've had these things happen to me over the last few years in my business but I've had other streams of income besides just one-on-one. My income didn't fluctuate and I was still able to take vacations, take care of my fiancée through cancer treatments and take care of myself after hip surgery.

One thing to note when you are offering one-on-one services is to charge what you're worth.

How much are you worth?

Well, most entrepreneurs I speak with aren't charging enough, put it that way.

I say charge as much as you can possibly say without stuttering. Yep. Because if you stutter then you show less confidence and people tend not to buy.

Business Models

So, charge as much as you can say confidently now and then raise your rates in a few months or after you get a few clients at this rate.

The other thing about offering one-on-one, is that you don't want to just charge hour by hour or group sessions together into a package of 12.

People want to buy a transformation, system or specific outcome, not number of sessions.

Think about the overarching result you will help your client achieve and how long will that take for most people to achieve?

If most won't achieve it without at least working with you for 6 months, then start there with your packages. Be realistic with the expectations and results based on effort. You can name your one-on-one program similar to a group program if you have a system you work with people on in your group. The one-on-one is just doing it faster or with more handholding and accountability perhaps.

Don't undervalue what people need and offer less time though just because you aren't sure if they can afford a longer time frame, that is not serving your client. You have to show the value of working with you for the right amount of time and how that will be more effective to getting them the desired result.

As for pricing one-on-one, this should be more than any group offer or online course as they're getting access to you, the expert.

Just to give you an example of how I changed my pricing over time, I started my business in 2002 doing the marketing for my clients at $59/hour. I quickly rose to $75/hour once I realized there weren't more hours to work. About three years in, I was charging $95/hour as I had traction with a full client base and more confidence. But I didn't know what I didn't know back then.

I had no idea that people who were doing what I was doing were making $250-500 per hour!! I didn't know this until I went to my first in person online business workshop. It was there that I was introduced to a whole new world of entrepreneurs making big money!

That's when I learned I could do more coaching and consulting for a higher rate per hour, rather than all the work for clients for less. That workshop changed my life!

If this is all new to you, then hopefully this book will change your life the same way!

Business Models

Group Programs

The good thing about having a group coaching program for example is that it leverages your time. You can host a live call on Zoom or other video/webinar software, or even in person. Then you can even record it and sell the recording of it to multiple people so that then it becomes a digital product or online course.

Back in the day of information products, we used to take those recordings and produce big binders with workbook and CDs! Now these typically lie digitally on your website or membership software.

Usually, the group program starts on one date and ends on another, that's what I call a "start stop program". Whereas a membership program or a continuity program is more of an ongoing program that never really stops unless someone decides to stop doing the program all together. People have to cancel in order to get out. You bill them automatically every month. These can have free levels or various paid levels; there's so many different options.

Rather than working with 10 people for 60 minutes each week or month one-on-one you can work with 10 people for 60-90 minutes together as a group every week. It's a lot less of your time to spend however, if you don't attract a large number of participants into your group, you could make a lot more money doing the one-on-one.

Note the pricing difference as follows:

- You have 10 One-on-One Clients working with you weekly for 6 months for 1 hour each week. You charge $200/hour, so your 6-month package is on or around $5,200 total per person. (I'll share how to do this differently but for this example.)

  That's $104,000 per year if you're full the whole year. It's also 10 hours per week of your time that you're spending with clients, plus whatever else they may need. (And of course, marketing and sales to fill those spots all year long.)

- Then you have 10 Clients in a Group program where you spend 1 Hour/week. That same program provides the same overall results the one-on-one does, and it's done over the same period perhaps, 6 months.

  You value your time the same, so $5,200 for those 26 hourly calls. Maybe a little more since you might have to serve them or do Q&A in an

Business Models

online membership group too perhaps. Let's say $6,000 total income divided by 10 people that's only $600 per participant.

But that's not a realistic expectation for someone to pay for a 6-month group program. The reality is that you could charge $5,200 or $6,000 for this group program, increasing your hourly value when you have 10 participants to $2,307 per hour!

This is why it's good to have a mix of different business models. You could do BOTH pretty easily with your time and make $224,000 per year with 10 clients one-on-one the whole year and 10 participants in your group that you run twice a year. That's with just working about 11-13 hours per week with clients.

That's also basing your worth/value at a low $200/hour! I'll bet you can say you're worth more than that now, right?

What's the reality of how easy or difficult it is to sell some of these business models you may ask?

Well, you usually need a lot more time to sell your group program than you think. So there's a ramp up sales period depending on how much it is. If it's a couple of hundred bucks or less than it might be three to four weeks in marketing. If it's more than that you're probably going to need more like five weeks to a few months to market and sell the spots. If it's $2,000 or more then you really want three months or so to sell it.

The best way to sell anyone into any program that is over $500 however is to have a private conversation with them – a sales conversation.

One of the biggest issues with a group program is you believing that participants will get what they want and need.

I had a hard time believing this when I first offered a group program, so much so that I threw in a few bonus one-on-one calls with me to make sure they got what they needed. The beauty of it all though is that you can do whatever you want and change it as you go!

Live Events

One of the business models that I love is hosting live, in person events. I've hosted short, 2-4 hour events, one day events but what I find works best are three day events.

Business Models

Events are designed not to necessarily make your money in the front end, on ticket sales. In the coaching industry, your big money is made in the back end by offering a high-end program during the event.

Getting butts in seats is the tough part about hosting a live event however. If you really want to get 50 or more people in the room, you'll have to bust your hump at other events to sell tickets or do lots of one-on-one connecting online to sell tickets.

It's not always easy to just send an email or two to your email list to fill the thing. It used to be! If you just want five or ten people, it's much more doable.

In fact, I've switched my in-person event strategy since the Pandemic. I did a few virtual events during that time too, sending the swag box and all in the mail. In the beginning, they worked ok to sell into other programs, but it's changed a lot now writing this in fall of 2023.

I don't rely on virtual events anymore. They can be good for list building but not as much for conversions for me. Some people are still finding success in them, it all depends on who is on your list and what you do to promote.

Instead, I'm starting to bring back small, higher end mastermind retreats. I'm calling them Lifestyle & Business Growth Retreats and I'm loving this model!

With events, you want to look at your cost analysis, so you know what it's going to cost you to run the event. Think about the kind of experience you want people to have and what you want to sell at the event in order to cover the costs and make a profit!

I used to hold my live events in a hotel conference room, but you certainly don't have to start there or hold your events there. Typically for your first event, I recommend finding a place that doesn't charge you such as a friend's conference room.

I really love to have staging and lighting and all that stuff but I rarely spring for that level of production. I used a stage when I did these but the hotel I used threw it in for me. When you run your own events, you have to get good at negotiating your contracts.

Now, with the mastermind retreats, I look for Airbnb homes and locations, I look for boutique hotels or those with a very nice conference room instead of a ballroom.

I've made a lot of mistakes in hosting live events in the past and I've spent a lot of money where I shouldn't have in that area. I learned from a lot of the big guys (and gals) who host 400-1200 person events and you don't want to compare yourself with what they do when you're just starting out, trust me. You don't just go blindly reserving a huge ballroom to fit 200 people on your first event. You could be lucky to get 30 people. Plan for smaller perhaps unless you have a big responsive following.

The marketing timeline for a 3-day event, regardless of the ticket price, could be 3-6 months out. But before you go planning an event, always start with what you'll sell in the back of the room first.

Memberships & Continuity

The one thing I wanted to mention about a continuity program which is basically a membership program is that typically members don't stick around that long.

Some people in the industry are kicking butt with their membership programs, whether for $5.95/month or $97/month, but this is NOT the norm. They take just as much time and effort to sell in my opinion than a $1,000 group program or a $10,000 one-on-one package.

Usually, members join with a special offer you might make such as, buy two months get one free or $1 for your initial month and then it's $47/month after that. They come in for that and then they cancel before the special ends or they stick around for a few months and leave. They often realize that they aren't going to take advantage of the benefits so they cancel.

With a membership program, high turnover is probable unfortunately. You'll also spend more time managing these clients so you may need someone to manage the program for you since at that price point it's not always worth your time to manage.

So be careful adding a membership program unless you really have at least one virtual assistant or person on your team who can help you manage some of the shopping cart stuff like declines and cancellations that go with that.

It's not as easy as you think to fill a couple of hundred people into membership programs. Often when people are cutting costs in their businesses and watching their wallet they will cut out all those little 10, 20, 40, or 50 dollar things that they're subscribed to.

I've launched and managed four membership programs over my journey as an entrepreneur, from very low end, $7/month to $25,000/year mastermind programs.

Business Models

The greatest number of members that I've ever gotten was 214 people in my $7/month International Entrepreneur Network, a group that I thought I would get thousands of people to join and stay in with all I was offering! I ran and promoted that heavily for two years too. You would think more would have joined and rarely would someone cancel. It offered three live Q&A Laser Coaching calls with me every single month after all! I was shocked.

Another group program I ran years ago, the Love & Money Club, was $47/month and 50 people was the most I ever had at one time over 3 years. It was a lot to manage too. People that pay the least, tend to often be the most demanding. Have you experienced that yet?

Masterminds

I've been running a mastermind program since 2009 and it's my favorite program to run. I love the clients who jump into these kinds of programs. They actually do the work. They come to the calls. They're more responsible, more interactive. Many of them stick around for 3 to 7 years too and they become great friends. Plus, they often bond well with each other at this level. They're my highest paying clients to boot.

It's where I can really give the best of me to those clients who really appreciate it most.

A mastermind is where I've also received the best mentoring and support to grow my own business! I've been a part of at least 7 different people's mastermind programs since 2006, investing over $250,000 to learn what I needed to know to grow my own business.

I recommend thinking about how you can have a higher end program like a mastermind too and what that looks like for you. You don't have to be teaching something relating to business in order to run a high end mastermind. It is good to have been a part of one or two first however so you can get ideas on how you want to run your own, plus how you don't.

What is a mastermind?

Mastermind groups offer a combination of brainstorming, education, peer accountability and support in a group setting to sharpen your skill set in a specific area. A mastermind group helps you and your mastermind group members achieve more success. Participants challenge each other to set powerful goals, support each other, and more importantly, to accomplish their goals.

Business Models

Through a mastermind group process, first you create a goal, then a plan to achieve it. The group helps you with creative ideas and wise decision-making. Then, as you begin to implement your plan, you bring both success stories and problems to the group.

In the coaching world, a mastermind program is typically a coach's highest end program. It's usually the thing they charge the most money for. It's also often the thing that will bring their clients the most transformation.

For me, I offer basically everything and the kitchen sink to members in my mastermind. Members get me one-on-one, on group coaching calls, in live events and private retreats plus they get pretty much all of my programs, products and services as additional, supplemental learning.

You can design your mastermind however you want. Mine has evolved a lot over time and the beauty is that I get to design it around how I prefer to work and around the type of lifestyle that I want to live. I've just revised it again with a new name and focus, the Jumpstart Your Next Level Mastermind. I'm so excited for this next level journey for me and my clients!

Honestly, this is a great business model to have for almost any business or industry. You just have to develop the confidence to know you're someone people will invest in and follow. The truth is though, they are investing in themselves via you. The support you give your members throughout the course of a program like this, often one year long, is exactly what a lot of people need.

Most people need more time for the transformation process plus it gives them time in case "life happens" and gets in the way to slow them down.

Another fun twist to how to charge for your mastermind that I learned and implemented years ago is tiered pricing. That means that the first year is more than the second year and perhaps the third year is even less. This helps the clients see the possibility of sticking around, making it easier to do so too.

For over 6 years I've been selling into my mastermind with this process and right from the beginning, members sign up for 2 or 3 years at one time, with one contract. I break up the payment plan into 24 or 36 monthly payments even so it's even easier for them to pay.

Why? Because I can and it's easier for them. It also provides you consistent income coming in every month when you do this... for 2 to 3 years! I highly recommend it.

The first year is more because that's also when the client needs the most support from you. As they go, they tend to use less and less one-on-one, so it frees up your time a bit but they're still getting huge value and accountability. It's a win-win for each party.

Paid Speaking

Speaking can either be a free marketing strategy or a paid business model. It can also be a pay to speak type of situation too however that's more like an advertising or marketing expense than a business model.

I've done all three but primarily I speak for free. There are a lot more opportunities to get in front of audiences with a free talk plus you can sell whatever you want in the back of the room or in the follow up if they don't allow selling. Speaking for free is technically a marketing strategy, not a business model.

To speak as a paid business model, you need a good plan. You also want to clearly identify which types of organizations, conferences or companies that you and your topic would be a good fit for.

The best way to market yourself as a paid speaker is the direct approach. Buy or gather a list of prospects, then contact them over time via direct mail and phone primarily. Many paid speakers also use LinkedIn to reach out to speaker bookers. And there are also some things such as speaker bureaus and speaker bookers who actually do the work to book you. Those are paid strategies. It does take some time and a lot of finesse.

It is good to put a price tag on your speaking just in case you get invited to speak to at big conference or for a company who has a budget for speakers and a lot of them do. You can always waive your fee to those who don't pay.

How much do you charge? It depends on what you speak on and for whom but charging $3,000-$10,000 is a general range. I am listed as a paid speaker on a few speaker directories for example and list myself for $10,000 per speech as a speaker. I also add that my fee is negotiable depending on what else is included or provided and where it is.

There are speaker directories, many of them charge, such as espeakers.com or speakerhub.com. I've been

Business Models

on both for years and not seen any invitations to speak, however.

Regardless, if you speak for free or a fee, you always want to negotiate having a table in the back of the room, maybe a way to have them buy copies of your book if you have one or ask to have your materials paid for. You never know what you can get until you ask!

There's a lot more to know about getting paid speaking gigs. However, one of the biggest mistakes I see when people go after getting booked is that they don't set their fee high enough. I always recommend to "start high, go low". That means you start off as high as you possibly can. Then there's room to negotiate down from there.

Jumpstart Your New Business Now!

CHARACTERISTICS OF SUCCESSFUL SPEAKERS

THEY DO NOT	THEY ARE	THEY
• Sit in Indecision	• Assertive in Actions	• Rely on & Trust Others to help & Support them
• Overthink things	• A Leader	• Always keep sight of the BIG PICTURE
• Get Squirreled	• A Delegator	
• Procrastinate	• Intuitive	
• Let Fear Get in the Way	• Highly Self-Motivated	• Are Constantly Learning
• Doubt their Actions & Decisions	• Observant	• Always think how to leverage & automate
• Sit and Wait until they Figure Something Out - They ask!	• Thoughtful	• Take Calculated Risks
	• Generous	• Invest Often in Themselves & their Businesses
	• Planners	
	• Organized	
• Make Excuses	• Determined	• Kick Fear & Doubt to the Curb when it Arises
• Ignore Advice from Mentors	• Extroverts & Introverts	
• Avoid Their Numbers or Tracking Stats	• Strong Willed	• Take ample time to Work ON Their Business Every Day/Week/Month
	• Thorough	
	• Selective on Where to spend their time/money	
• Waste Time		• Do not attend events that won't be productive
• Avoid Conflict	• Open to opportunities	

(C) COPYRIGHT 2021 K. SAWA MARKETING INT'L INC.
WWW.JUMPSTARTYOURBIZNOW.COM

Do-It-Yourself Products / Courses

Basically, this is packaging up your knowledge or expertise in some way. It could be written or recorded in audio or video format or even transcribed so that people can consume it later without you being there.

I recommend entrepreneurs record EVERYTHING you do and teach if you possibly can. You never know how you can monetize it later or in other ways.

It can be a digital download like an eBook or MP3, it can be a digital workbook and video course delivered via a webpage or course software, it can be a flash drive mailed out with everything in one place, or it

Business Models

can be any combination you can imagine. There's all kinds of ways to package your expertise.

Extra revenue streams like this can add hundreds or thousands of dollars to your bottom line each month, even if you just sell a $10 book, a $27 training, a $7 5-day challenge, a $197 starter kit or a $1,997 home study program like my Jumpstart Your Business in 90 Days used to sell for online.

If you aren't sure what to create, record or sell online, you just need to brainstorm it with me! You may just not see what's possible. You also can start by doing some webinars, teaching stuff you share with clients, and then recording those classes. Many, if good, you can then sell right away!

I love helping people pull out their "signature system" or content like this. Start thinking about the "process" you take people through, what steps do you take with them? That's a great place to start.

One of the most challenging businesses I've worked with to create a do-it-yourself product for was with a wedding flower designer client. She was so tired of just doing wedding after wedding after wedding after wedding and she wanted to do something different to provide more residual income for her retirement.

We spent three hours brainstorming over the course of three different calls to see what else she could do that could relate to the wedding flower business.

We threw around ideas on all kinds of different business models like I've been talking about here and we finally came up with the PERFECT THING – The Do It Yourself Wedding Flower Guide!

The Do It Yourself Wedding Flower Guide became a combination product with eBook, Resources Checklist of where to find lower priced flowers and everything needed to create your own wedding flowers plus a series of videos on how to create them all. It really was a brilliant idea and the client loved it.

There are people who wouldn't hire her anyway because they wanted to do their own wedding flowers so why not create a resource to help that target market accomplish their goal?

We basically took her knowledge of how to design bouquets, corsages and table decorations and showed how to do it all yourself. It was everything you needed in regards to creating your own flowers for a wedding and how to do it all with different variations and all the different types of flowers to use. It was the

Business Models

most innovative thing I'd seen for that kind of a business.

She videotaped it all in her home, wrote out the eBook and resources list, and to be competitive for do-it-yourselfers, we priced it at just $97!

My client sold them online, spoke around the country about it and got a bunch of publicity with it too.

What did that do for her? Well, she had a great time for the next couple years selling it and promoting it and then just like most business owners, this idea evolved. Her business evolved, she evolved and you want to be open to the evolution of you and your business too.

You just don't know what you don't know and it is worth talking to someone like me.

Retail Store or Brick and Mortar

Everyone knows what this type of business is but when do you know when NOT to open one?

Let me share a story about a gal who attended one of my live seminars; we'll call her Susan. Susan came to my event to learn how to open a florist. Susan loved to arrange flowers for friends and family events, weddings and more.

This was back in 2009, florists were still thriving and not yet taken over by grocery stores or 1-800-Flowers.

The problem for Susan was her big picture vision and goal was to have kids soon. She'd just gotten married and they were planning on kids in the very near future.

What do you think the "reality check" for her was in regards to opening this type of retail business?

Running a retail store of any kind is pretty much a 24/7 thing, at least in the beginning. You have the build out, the pre-marketing, the buying of inventory, hiring staff, training staff, and staffing it during business hours hoping no one calls in sick. Then there is additional work behind the scenes and after hours to manage the books, deal with vendors, inventory, store or shop upkeep and maintenance. When was she going to realistically have time to start a family much less take maternity leave?

Once she really learned what it would take to start THIS kind of business, she backed off immediately. She realized that she didn't know what she didn't know and was glad to have invested in my event to learn it all and save her years of struggling and probably hundreds of thousands of dollars.

Business Models

Now, not all retail businesses are a bad idea. But please do your homework. Learn everything you can about the type of business you want to open. Talk with other business owners who own the same type of business. Interview them and pick their brain on the pros and cons.

Be realistic about what it will really take financially to open, run, market and grow. I hear stories all the time that build outs take double what people originally budget for, money wise and time wise. Then there's the marketing. It's not enough to just have a great location anymore. You have to give people incentive to come in and you must have a monthly marketing budget.

There are franchise opportunities for brick and mortar which is becoming the easiest type of brick and mortar to open frankly. It comes with systems, operation manuals on how to do everything. It comes with instruction on how to hire, find and manage vendors, market and more.

Some people have ideas of the most quaint or perfect in person business though sometimes and you just can't deter them. If this is you, please hire a business coach or consultant before you start so you can plan for the unexpected and for the things you don't know you don't know.

Online Store

Often when entrepreneurs want to start a retail store they think, "I'll just start an online store so I don't need a big start up budget".

They think it will be so easy to sell stuff online since it's super easy to create a website these days. While that's true, the problem with this is that it's like opening a retail store in a part of town that's abandoned and no one ever even drives by.

You've got to do even more marketing with an online store than a brick and mortar location. Yes, the "build out" is a lot less expensive and yes, you could drop ship your products too depending on what you're selling but by no means is this an EASY business model to make money at quickly.

Let me share a story about my pet sitter who decided she wanted to sell products. We'll call her Nancy.

Nancy was already making pretty good money sitting for people's pets in her own home. She did pet visits and walking too but the bulk of her money was for watching dogs by the day. At any given time she had four or five dogs in her home besides her own.

Business Models

It's actually a logical next step for Nancy to sell and recommend pet products and she actually did set up that side of the business in a very low-maintenance, low-cost manner.

Nancy didn't decide to just sell one or two pet products, she created a whole online pet store investing quite a bit of money. She ran that for a few years, promoting the products to her current clients but never really did enough to really make a lot of money with that side of her business because she didn't do any online mass marketing. Therefore, she hardly had any traffic to her online store.

Plus, a few years later, Nancy found a new passion and became a certified life coach. As I said, you want to be open to the evolution of you and your business.

Here's a big revelation for you at this moment I'm sure: It's okay to CHANGE YOUR MIND.

I've worked with or had discussions with entrepreneurs who wanted to start or were running businesses online selling products such as:

- Baby strollers
- Guns
- Pet products, food, clothing

- Handbags
- Jewelry
- Handmade crafts
- Art

I don't want to deter you from starting this kind of business but please make sure you set realistic expectations and you have months of funding for your basic expenses in the start-up phase. Get help to set this up so you're doing it the right way from the start.

One more type of online business model is selling on Amazon. It's a relatively popular concept these days. I know at least three people doing this model right now but only one is hugely successful at it. The one person who is successful at it then also created a group program which turned home study and membership on how to sell on Amazon. She created four or five revenue streams from this once she started making money and realizing how it worked. She saw the potential for teaching others. We call that a "train the trainer" type of program.

A "train the trainer" program is one of the most common types of business models most entrepreneurs can start as you already know something about something. Package that expertise into one of the business models I've mentioned before and sell that if you're not sure what to do.

Affiliate Marketing

Affiliate marketing is where you promote and sell other people's stuff and make money on it.

I highly recommend you do this. There are products, businesses, services that we all believe in, use and recommend. Many of them you can make commissions on if you refer people to go buy them. It's a relatively easy business model to implement and costs the least amount of money for you.

All you have to do is ask or search on the company's website for their affiliate program, partner program or contact them to find out how you can do this.

Typically, you'll get a unique URL that you can share with people and when they click and buy, it's tracked back to you. Sometimes it's a bit more complicated than that but still worth it if you can make money from just a recommendation or referral.

What would you promote and sell?

Well, Nancy the pet sitter sells pet products, clothes and food.

A massage therapist could sell lotions, massage equipment for home use, essential oils, massage chairs, other health supplements possibly and even more.

A dentist could sell teeth whitening kits, or make commissions on referrals to Orthodontists and other professionals.

A fitness trainer could sell protein shakes, supplements, vitamins, weight loss products, exercise equipment for home use, referrals to physical therapists or health coaches, and more.

I share resources with affiliate links to things such as CRM and shopping cart software, email marketing services, other techy tools, Virtual Assistants, other professionals that work with my types of clients, Amazon products that I recommend and more. In fact, I have a page on my website dedicated to those recommended resources here if you want to see how I set it up:

https://jumpstartyourbiznow.com/recommended-resources/

Every now and again, I run across an entrepreneur however whose main goal is to only promote other people's products, nothing else; they want to be an affiliate marketer. The problem with this thought

Business Models

process is that there's no trust built up yet or connection with the audience that you're building. Setting up an affiliate marketing business like this to promote a lot of different things seems like an easy way to make money on other people's stuff but typically you won't do well because you're not known for anything.

Now, I do know some affiliate marketers who are very profitable and successful but they are usually doing their own niche business too. It's easier to share complimentary services or people with the clients or followers you have who like trust and connect with you already than to sell random things cold to those who just found you.

The goal of your website is to build your list. The only reason people want to get on your list is because they like what you're saying and like what you're doing and they trust you. But then if all you do is market other people's things to your list and nothing of your own, people won't follow you for very long. This is my personal opinion. I think that's not the route to go.

I think a lot of people do that and latch onto those opportunities because they don't see what they have that they can sell. They don't see what's possible for them or they're not confident in their own abilities yet.

Therefore, I think it's important for you to figure out what you can sell first, what type of business you can run for yourself. Then if it makes sense to add other business models or sell other people's stuff that is complementary to what you're doing that's fine.

As a business coach, I recommend certain software, shopping carts and email marketing systems. I get paid commission on the things that people sign up for through my affiliate links. I would recommend them anyway but if I can make money doing it then that's smart marketing.

As a side note to the online business or affiliate models, there are a lot of websites that have the Google ads all over them. That's a primary revenue stream for them. This type of marketing used to be a lot more popular with even the smallest entrepreneur but isn't as much anymore. Usually just the larger companies or organizations run ads on their websites. I'm a member of a few organizations who do this such as the Women Speakers Association for example.

Look around on the websites of organizations you belong to and see if they have ads running on them.

Business Models

Your chamber of commerce sites often does. Heck, even YouTube videos have ads on them, and you can make money on those ads if you're big enough on YouTube with enough views each month.

Network Marketing

Do you want to know the REAL pros and cons of network marketing?

I've seen thousands of people sell network marketing products and programs, I've even promoted some myself.

The main pro is, and what those companies tell you most is, that you want to join to earn great residual income. Yes, it's true, that is a huge reason to join a network marketing business. We all want residual income for life. That would just set us all up to retire happily and do whatever we want, right?

The statistic however that I've heard is that less than 3% of the people doing network marketing businesses ever get beyond $100,000/year in income.

I'm pretty sure that I've only met less than ten or so people making big money from their network marketing business. Many people doing those types of business models have other business models too; it's not all that they do to create their income.

The main con, and what those companies don't tell you is that you need to get good at selling and marketing. Yes, it's vital that you're super passionate about whatever the products are that you're selling. But it's really not about the products. It's about getting good at sales and marketing activities. That's the only way you'll ever make any money doing this business model. It's not as easy as they make it sound.

So if you're NOT excited about selling something that you're passionate about, then don't get into a network marketing business.

The goal of a network marketing business is to get a huge line of distributors underneath you also actively working the business. To find that many highly motivated people is not easy. Then you must motivate them too so you become a coach in the process. The ones doing well hold weekly meetings with their downlines and share resources and best practices all typically for free.

Realistically, if you are good (or get good) at the sales and marketing stuff, it might take three to five years to really build up a good revenue stream for yourself. The most I usually see however is still only about $3,000 per month.

Business Models

If you're trying to leave your job and build a business on the side to replace your income, this is not the business model that I recommend.

If you do other business models and want to add a network marketing product onto what you're already doing and making money at, that is what I recommend. Similarly to the examples mentioned when I talked about online businesses:

- A fitness trainer could sell Isagenix
- A hair stylist could sell Monat
- A massage therapist could sell doTerra
- A health coach could sell Juice Plus
- A business coach could sell Send Out Cards
- An image consultant could sell Cabi

All of those examples have their main revenue stream as their main business then something they can sell in the back end to clients as supplemental income.

I still don't recommend you add on these types of products until you have a smooth-running moneymaking business model first.

And which network marketing business is the best one? Or which one should you join if you were going to do this type of business model?

That's hard to say. Some of them change rapidly, some go out of business. Others are tried and true staples that you hear about all the time such as Mary Kay.

Some people believe that you only make money with these if you get in on the ground floor of the company and you're one of the first couple dozen or so people doing the business. That's when you can build the biggest downlines.

I'm not an early adopter however, so I wouldn't risk getting into a business like that too early on. I like to see it become a proven system and company first.

One thing I definitely would recommend is only do one where you're extremely passionate about whatever it is that you're selling please. People detect when you aren't passionate and they definitely won't buy from you then.

If you're already doing a network marketing business then let's figure out one of these other business models that you can use for faster cash and more money in the door up front.

Business Models

Certification Program or Licensing

These two types of business models are when you turn that "train the trainer" program into one that you can sell the rights to basically. Others can then sell your signature system and train people on it or help people through it.

I have a few friends who've turned their signature systems, their main training programs, into either a certification program or they've licensed it to have others teach it.

I'm not opposed to this type of program, it definitely leverages your time and expertise.

It's not for everyone either however, there's a lot more legal work involved and depending on which state or country you're in, there could be other logistics. You want to make sure you keep your brand intact with the licensing.

I was thinking about licensing my Jumpstart Your Marketing Follow Up System to other business and marketing coaches but I never went through with it. Once I looked into starting the process, it was just too cumbersome and at that time, I needed to generate consistent cash flow first so taking on a project like that was not good timing for me.

EXERCISE: Really think about which of these business models (or others too) will fit the kind of lifestyle that you desire.

Don't choose ones that will take up too much of your time for example if you only wish to work 20 hours a week. Don't choose ones that require travel for example if you really want to stay close to home and your family.

Be careful with this process, many entrepreneurs choose the wrong business models right from the beginning then struggle to make them work.

Keep in mind, I developed a private page just for those of you who have this book with opportunities for discounted calls with me as well as many other free and low-priced resources, videos, trainings, checklists and more. You can find all of this online at www.JumpstartYourBizNow.com/JumpstartBookResources.

Business Models

> "TO ANSWER THE QUESTION, WHAT SHOULD YOU CHARGE? WHAT IS THE HIGHEST POSSIBLE NUMBER PER HOUR YOU CAN THINK OF AND SAY WITHOUT STUTTERING. THAT'S YOUR GOING RATE UNTIL YOU CAN SAY HIGHER!" ~ KATRINA SAWA

Chapter 9

Time to Sell

"Charge as much as you can say without stuttering."
*~ **Katrina Sawa***

What are you REALLY Selling?

What are you really selling, besides the unique product or service that you're thinking in this minute?

I'll tell you.

You're selling the TRANSFORMATION or outcome. You're also selling YOURSELF. Your ideal prospects need to like, trust and connect with you in order to even consider buying from you or becoming a customer.

It's important to remember that EVERYONE is NOT your customer. Some will, some won't, so what? Keep this on top of your mind as you go through your day-to-day activities, or your head trash could take over and really let you feel down and depressed when you hear a lot of "nos".

So, what's the transformation your ideal target customer will experience by using or buying your product or service?

You want to sit down and write out or describe the outcome after they hire you or buy from you or use you or work with you.

- What will they have experienced?
- What will they be feeling?
- What will their results be?
- What will they walk away with?
- What will it do for them, their family, their life, their business, and their ultimate lifestyle?

If you're a health coach teaching weight loss for example:

- Are they going to have clear steps on what to do to change their eating habits?
- Are they going to have a meal plan to follow?
- Will they be able to make smarter shopping decisions?

Time to Sell

- Will they be motivated to exercise?
- Will they lose up to 20 pounds?
- Will they have more time with their family?
- Will they be able to get off certain medications?
- Will they feel better and have more energy?

These are the scenarios that you're selling. These are the things you say in a networking event when someone asks you what you do.

What does your product or service include?

This is where you talk about the features or components of what you're selling. For example:

If you offer a group program

- Is it four weeks, six weeks or three months?
- Are there live training calls or recordings?
- Is there an online membership area with additional resources or will you be emailing content to members?
- Will you offer some sort of access to you for questions or no access?
- Will they receive a 24-page workbook?

- Will you be bringing in outside experts to teach bonus classes?

When you're deciding what to include in your product, program or service you want to think about 3 things:

- Is this the best way for my customers to consume this information? Is this the way THEY want to get access to it?
- Does this work for me and my lifestyle?
- Can it be priced well enough to make it profitable for me?

Two of the biggest reasons I see a lot of entrepreneurs NOT creating group programs is because they:

1. Aren't sure if their customers will receive the same value or get the same result.
2. Aren't sure how to create it, develop the curriculum or run a group program.

This is a shame really, but I totally understand. I too, had a problem creating my first group program. I'd been working only one-on-one for many years and my clients got really great results that way.

Time to Sell

I wasn't sure if I put them into a group that they'd actually get what they needed to move forward in their business.

I also wasn't really feeling motivated to go create a bunch of curriculum.

Then one of my mentors said the magic words to me: "You want to build the plane while you're flying it."

That phrase changed my life.

What that means is that you want to sell the program BEFORE you create it. You want to do it live with paid participants while you create the curriculum. It makes it a whole lot easier to get the curriculum developed for one thing because you have people who've paid for it already so you've got an obligation to them to produce it.

Secondly, if you sell it first, then you know it's what people want. If you don't, and you go off creating something you think people need, then they may not want it when you turn around to try to sell it later.

That's just using a group program for an example but it is one of the business models that is easiest for most entrepreneurs to use.

I had a hard time creating the handouts for my programs, especially the one associated with my

Jumpstart Your Business in 90 Days Home Study Program. I only created them one or two days prior to each call where I had to walk my paying clients through the content and exercises.

The handouts were good too! I was shocked but they were exactly what people needed. I was just scared that they wouldn't be when the idea first came to me. I had to sell it then trust that I would produce the right results.

I bet that this will happen for you as well.

Another suggestion for you, when you're trying to figure out what to include in your own programs, products and services, make sure you've been in other people's programs before, or purchased some of their home study programs, you've seen and experienced examples to give you ideas. It's really helpful to model after other people's programs when you're getting started.

Choosing the Name

How do you choose what to name your product or service? This is a huge issue for many entrepreneurs.

I say, name it whatever sounds good to you today. You can always change it.

Time to Sell

If you wait too long to figure out the name or stay stuck on the name, you'll never make money at it so stop it. Remember, whatever you name it, use the hot buttons and your target market's words, not yours.

After you name it, then you have to price it, market it and sell it.

What's a good tagline or headline for the marketing of your product? What will make your target market STOP and read an email, webpage, flyer, etc.?

Think about it and write down some ideas now.

You need to position you and your product so that it's memorable and people find you online and want what you have to offer. You have to brand you, your product or your company.

You want to be thinking about what makes you different. Why are you different than others in your industry?

What is your business' unique competitive advantage or unique selling proposition? That is what you want to think about branding or highlighting.

Think about what you are an expert in and how you do things different. It doesn't matter that there are thousands of other health coaches out there for example, you do it different. You only need a small percentage of the people in the world to work with you anyway. You can break out and be the innovator in your industry.

Remember to think big when deciding on your offerings. If you don't have a $10,000 or $20,000 program then you'll never sell one, right? Create a high end offering if it fits with what you do... talk about it with people so you get more confident with offering something outside of your comfort zone.

Are you curious about what to include in a high-end program? Check out this chart for ideas but you can do whatever you want!

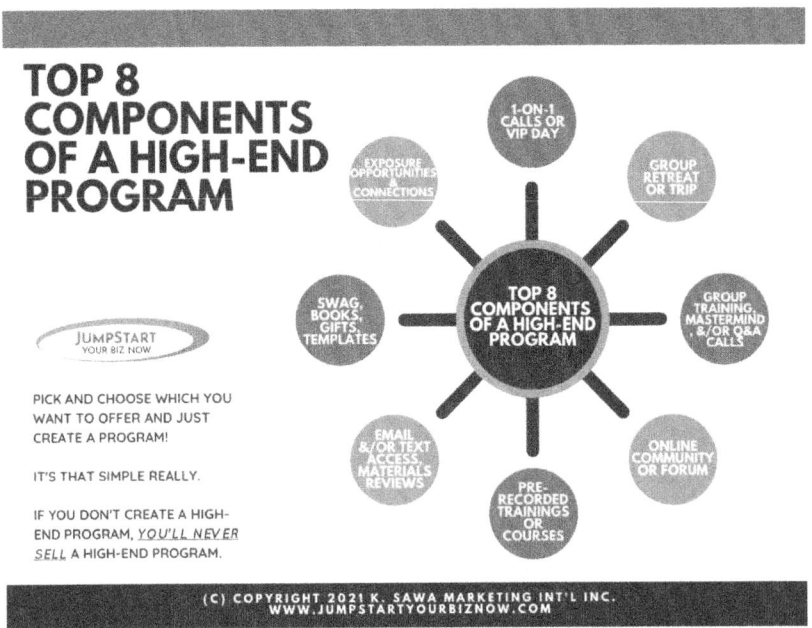

Exercise: Outline your product funnel and what all you are going to offer so you have a visual. Then break down how many of each product or service you believe you can easily sell each month.

Multiply that by the price you're planning on charging and see if the total adds up to your "need number".

If it does not, then you know you need to reevaluate something in your funnel, either a business model or pricing.

Here's an example of what offerings a coach or consultant might put in their funnel in order by price:

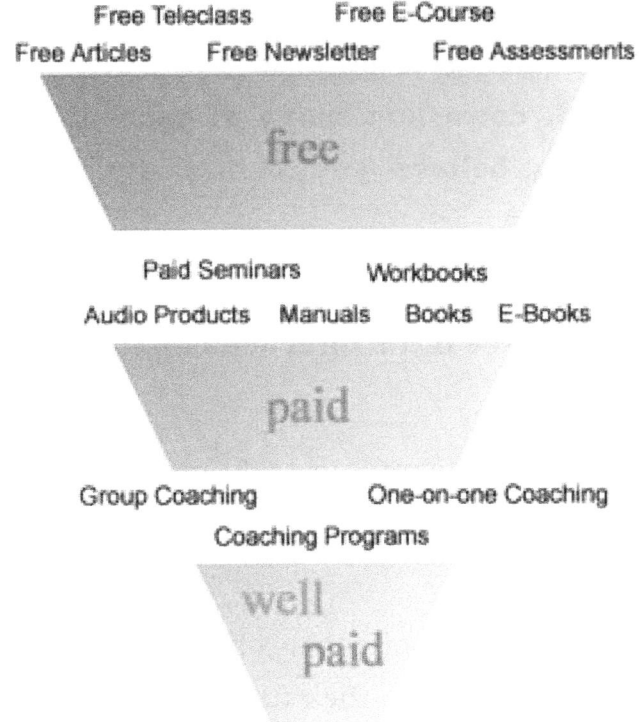

Closing the Sale

After you figure out what exactly you're selling, what's included, how much it costs and who it's for, then we need to help you sell more of it!

What would you do in this scenario?

- If you *had* to create $10,000 in 30 Days, what would be your plan?
- If your kid, parent, spouse, or loved one suddenly needed a necessary, life-saving

Time to Sell

surgery that cost $10,000, how would you create those funds if you didn't have them in savings or on a credit card?

Those circumstances might ignite a fire under you to go make money or sales, wouldn't it?

If you're a true entrepreneur, you wouldn't stress, you'd just go sell more products, programs and services!

When "life happens", let's face it, we often have to dive in and sell more to ramp back up quickly. You can do this!

When you how to make money, how to sell effectively, then you can do it whenever and wherever you are.

If you plopped me in a city where I knew no one and there was no internet, I would know how to go get clients and make sales. Would you? *Without the internet?*

I want to get you thinking about making sales consistently and with more ease so you can create a business where you can count on a certain level of revenue coming in every month.

Whether you're an entrepreneur, a sales associate, or an employee, you can always affect your moneymaking ability. And you can't rely on social media or the internet for sales; it's just too busy. That doesn't mean sales won't come from there, but you still have to master your sales and selling ability.

Making more money and jumpstarting your sales requires three things:

1. The confidence to go after what you want.
2. The opportunities available to you.
3. The skills to know how to do it, whatever *it* is.

I'm sharing more about selling in one's business, but you can apply much of this to other jobs where you have to do your own client generation, or even the sales and closing strategies with your children and family!

Generally, I'm talking about selling one-to-one here, although of course you can sell from the stage or through a virtual event as a speaker, and you can generate sales from people who land on your website. But where you'll sell tens of thousands of dollars consistently will most likely be in one-on-one sales conversations.

In order to Jumpstart Your Sales Conversations, you will need to hone your skills and business strategies around the following four areas:

Time to Sell

1. Fill your calendar with sales calls and appointments. Do you know how to do that, or do you have effective systems for people to get on your calendar virtually? If you have to touch and correspond with each and every lead or prospect who comes your way, you won't be talking with enough people. It's a numbers game, it always has been. And now, more than ever, with the expansive number of places online where your prospects are looking daily, you have to hook them in wherever they see you or find you. You have to have amazing systems in place and attention-grabbing copy or wording to make them stop and pay attention. Then, you have to hold their attention long enough and get them curious enough to want to know more. You have to make it easy for them to sign up to talk with you. In my experience, having reviewed thousands of entrepreneurs' websites and lead generation processes, the majority of people do not do this well enough to be effective.

2. Know how to dance in those conversations with objections, questions about pricing, and incentives to take action today. You can't be afraid to share the reasons why someone

should work with you or buy your product. You can't be afraid to ask them if they're ready to sign up, or if they have any more questions before signing up. You want to be comfortable talking about money, their money, and how they can find the resources to invest. You don't want to be stuck without an answer or a response to whatever concerns they may have. Being prepared with the answer to any question or situation is key. Having bonuses or incentives are a great way to get prospective clients to commit today rather than "think about it," especially if the offers are juicy enough. Try using bonuses before discounts—although discounts work well, too. Give a time limit for them to decide before the discount or bonus is gone. See what happens!

3. Be assertive and consultative, not salesy and sleazy, and remember to ask them to take the next step. Be curious and interested in solving their problem. Ask questions of them to build rapport and trust so they feel like you understand them. I even share tips I've shared with others if a certain topic comes up; I don't hold back all my ideas. I want to make them aware that I already have a plan for growing

their business quickly. Once they say yes, I even get them started on their next steps right then and there; I don't make them wait.

4. Have the right offerings and business models or know how to develop custom packages on the fly. Know your limits for pricing, the lowest you can go, or what you can throw in for bonuses to get someone to act today. Start with your highest offerings that are a good fit, then go down from there. Don't start low and go up—that never works! Have a way for someone to try you out if they aren't willing to go all in with a larger or longer package. I offer a three- or four-call package if someone is interested but not quite ready to dive into my six-month or annual program just yet. Have a way to take the money today, too, even if you make up a new package. Get the technology in place to make it easy for you to ask for their credit card on the spot; don't leave the sign up in their hands to be finalized in the follow-up.

Are you effective in the majority of your sales transactions and conversations now? Do you close the business, make the sale, or land the client in MOST instances? If not, it could be time you enlisted a script—or at least a list of questions to ask, points to cover, responses to common objections, and offers you can make. That's how I got started, and sometimes I still keep some notes handy.

Scripting is the best way to help you overcome some of the biggest frustrations in the sales process. This is why my coaching clients record me during our calls together. I'm very good with the words. They like to use my words and phrases during their sales conversations, and also in their emails, marketing materials, webpages, and videos.

Sales scripting can help you build trust easily, avoid losing sales by delivering options prematurely, and overcome anxiety or fear about what to say. It can ensure that your sales conversations always follow a persuasive sequence, steering a path to a strong close.

Here are my 5 Favorite Closing Techniques:

1. Optional Close – Give them choices, like: "Do you want this, or that? Six months, or a year? Start now, or in 30 days? Pay with PayPal, or with credit card?" Give them options instead of just "yes" or "no."

Time to Sell

2. Assume the Sale – Assume they are going to buy, because why else would they come to a call with you—and be shocked if they tell you no.

3. Fear of Loss – Make them feel like they will really be missing out if they do not buy from you. What would they do instead? This product or service is going away.

4. Sense of Urgency – Create a sense of urgency. Make them feel that they need to hurry up and buy before the product and/or service is gone, the price increases, bonuses go away, or because there's a limited quantity or seating available.

5. The Takeaway Close or Indifference – Make them feel that it doesn't matter to you whether they buy or not. Explain that it's not a big deal and that it's up to them.

Jumpstart Your New Business Now!

I've listed all 8 Sales Strategies in this handy graphic.

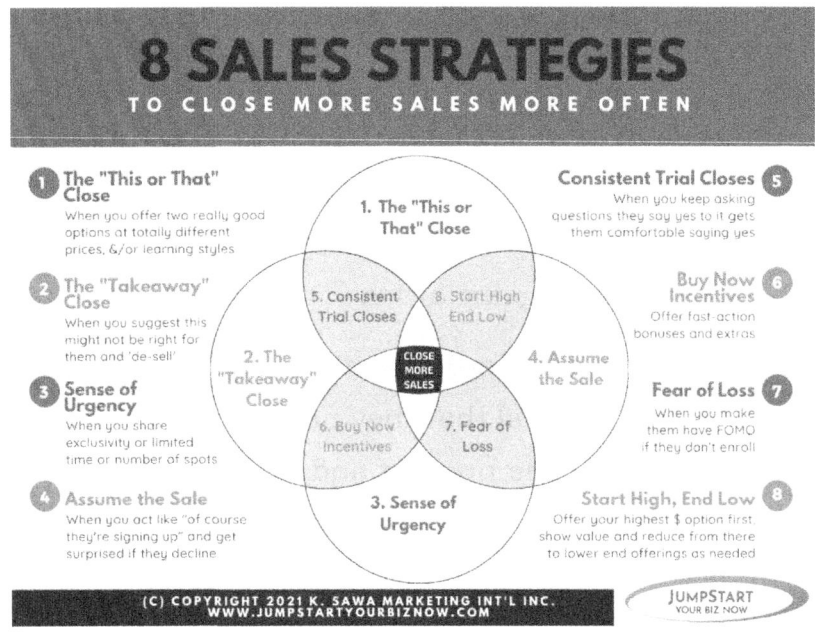

Chapter 10

Online Set-Up

"Your website needs to be the HUB of your business."
~ Katrina Sawa

I'm going to touch on what you need to know to provide your product or service online these days.

My goal is also to share the most affordable way possible with you in setting up your business online.

For those of you who want to sell products and services from your website I will address that in a moment.

But first, for those of you reading that don't think you will sell online or have anything to sell online, please read on and reconsider that thinking.

Plus, setting your business up for success online is not always about selling online, it can include setting up the systems and functionality so you can stop working so hard.

You see, one of the biggest things that has allowed me to reach so many people and get so much done are my systems. My systems run in and through my website. My website is the hub of my business, and it should be the hub of yours too.

This chart shows an example of a process that you might take a lead or prospect through, some call this your "funnel" but I consider this a strategy or process for your customer journey.

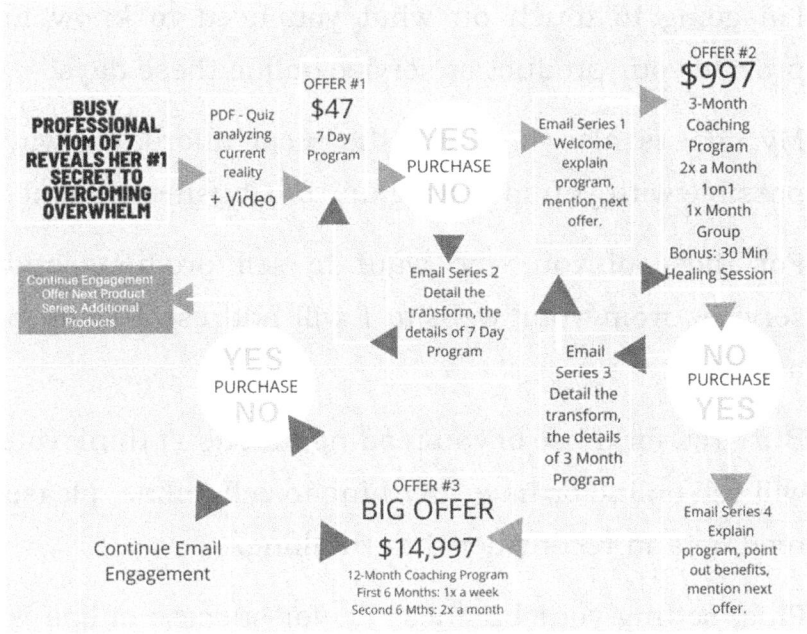

Why, if you're a therapist, CMT, dentist, or dog sitter would you need systems of this level?

- For a WOW customer experience

Online Set-Up

- For less hands-on, manual labor on the part of you or your team

- For new client intake, client management, client exiting or cancellation

- To make it easier for the customers to buy or get information anytime they want, or when they land on your website. (You're not going to answer the phone at midnight, are you?)

- For better follow up after visits

- For upsells and ongoing services and offers

Now, I'm not going to tell you exactly which online technology or systems you need in this book. If I did that I'd be doing you a disservice because not all businesses need the same thing.

I can give you some indication however as to if this, then that. If you have a certain scenario then I recommend specific action.

You see, even if you just sell one-on-one services and only to local people, you will benefit from running credit cards through your website and handling the filling in of new client forms online as well.

Much of what can be done for you especially will be to save you time managing your business and your clients. It can also sort and prequalify your leads so you spend less time talking with people who aren't ready to buy now and more time with who are. To prequalify prospects before they get to your calendar to schedule a free consult for example, you can add a video identifying who the perfect client is and is not, a form they have to fill out answering many questions, or even an application process to determine if they are a good fit. You don't want to waste your time with the wrong people.

I know some of this sounds a little impersonal, but it doesn't have to be. This depends on how you write and connect in the content of your site and your follow up.

Copywriting is a huge skill that you really want to learn to master. Most entrepreneurs I meet are NOT good at writing content for their own websites or marketing copy and emails either. This is a learned skill but you can learn it. You must learn it or hire it out but it's cheaper in the long run if you can learn how to get good at this. I can help.

Here's a list of the types of technology and systems you may need or want to set up in your business depending on what you're selling.

Online Set-Up

- A very functional and professionally built website. I wouldn't recommend a build-your-own-template site these days if you really want to get a lot of traffic without paying for it. The web builder templates are ok to use temporarily but won't help you attain more freedom in the long run. They just aren't as efficient or practical.

- A shopping cart and merchant services company so you can take credit cards online and track your sales too. PayPal is a temporary solution but it is not good long term because it doesn't track your sales well or act as your database or CRM. You want an all-inclusive system. Stripe is a common credit card processor that works with many website platforms and database management software.

- Email marketing software. That can be the same as the above shopping cart software or a stand-alone CRM, many are all-in-one options for these days though. When you're just starting out though, there are options for all of what you need for just $28/month. I wouldn't get caught up in $200-300/month software too early on before you make some consistent money, that's a mistake I see. Whatever system you use for emailing has to be through a spam-compliant service. You also can't just add anyone to your email list. You have to use an approved system to send emails to your list of subscribers that has an unsubscribe link and physical address in every email you send, or it's considered spam.

- A blog with posts relevant to your topic.

- Funnels, landing pages or lead magnets – you may have heard of these terms and wonder if you need them or not. You do. But you don't necessarily need the costly monthly service fees that some services charge to put your pages on their servers. You can build funnels and landing pages or free gift opt in pages on your main website. You could use other software to do it, but it's not required, and many people will try to sell you their solution that costs an added fee every month. It's not necessary.

- Social Media – as for all the social platforms out there, they are what you use for marketing. They are not where you put your website, webpages or secured database. You do not

Online Set-Up

control any social media website therefore you do not want to rely on any of them to be where you keep your followers or subscribers. You always want to entice them OFF of social media on to your website and get them on your email list or in your database so you can continue to market to them. And which social media platforms to be on depends on which you prefer, your ideal clients and where they hang out, and how much you do on them depends too on your ideal lifestyle vision and goals. You don't have to do it all!

- A Zoom account is pretty standard these days and useful for one-on-one client calls, sales conversations, webinars, and collaboration calls with referral sources. I highly recommend recording everything.

Here is a list of things you may need to write or generate content for to have on your website or to follow up and talk with leads:

- Sales/Squeeze/Opt-in pages
- Product images, logos and online graphics
- Autoresponder emails
- Email blasts and Email newsletters

Jumpstart Your New Business Now!

- Develop website and new pages often
- Direct Mail Follow Up
- Blog Posts/Tweets
- Articles/Videos/Content for social media
- Order Forms in print and online
- Free consult questionnaires or quizzes and assessments
- Free gift on your website
- Follow Up Templates
- Marketing Plan
- Marketing Materials
- Giveaway in Person
- Curriculum for programs or Signature System
- FAQ page
- About page and bio for giving to podcast hosts
- Speaking topics and descriptions if you plan to speak plus a speaker sheet that lists them
- Privacy Policy and Terms for your website – required by law by the way!
- Tradeshow Display/Banner/Signs

Online Set-Up

These are all the things I can think of that you might need to create in the first one to three years of your business.

Now, if you've already been running a business successfully for quite some time, then you want to use this as a guide to see if you have all these pieces in place. Do you?

I know you may not feel comfortable acting like a salesperson and you also may not feel comfortable pushing your product or service, but if you don't do it and you don't have a sales team - *WHO WILL DO IT??*

Writing copy for your website, emails, social media profiles and marketing is the only way to convey what it is that you do and how you can help. Remember though that you are selling the "transformation", not just a product or service.

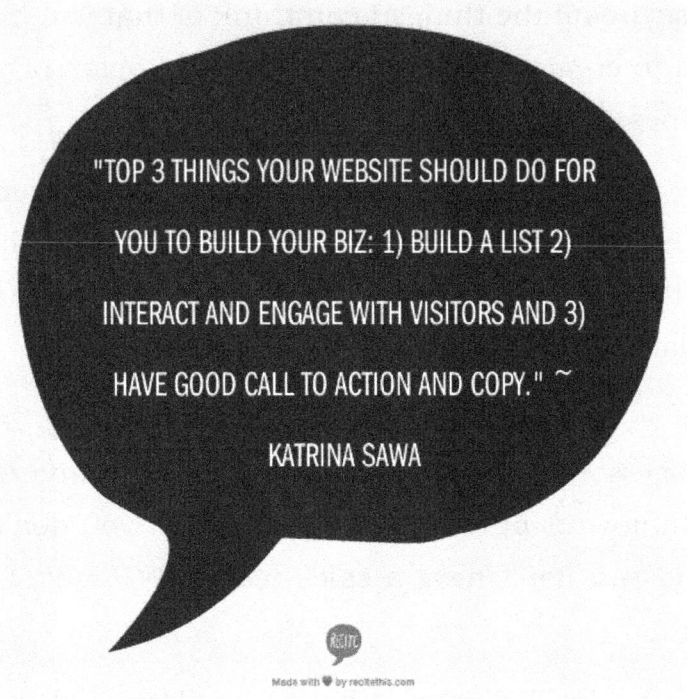

Possible Components/Pages of Your Website:

- Squeeze/Opt-in pages (also known as lead magnets or funnels)
- Home
- About
- Contact
- Services / coaching main page
- Inside sales pages, one for each product, program or service that you offer online

Online Set-Up

- Products / store main page
- Free resources / articles / free gifts
- Recommended vendors or resources
- Blog
- Testimonials
- Videos
- Media / In the News
- Speaking
- Events / calendar / workshops / webinars
- Membership sales page and/or backend for members access only
- Affiliate sign up and/or backend for resources
- Newsletter sign up or archives
- Free Quiz or assessment
- Free or paid initial consult / strategy session
- Portfolio or client list
- Terms / Policies / Legal Disclaimer – this is required by law, get help to do this right!
- FAQ

- Thank you pages – these are the delivery pages for your products and services, what do people need to know or receive once they buy or sign up? You put that on a hidden thank you page, not in your site's navigation.

There are more free resources and trainings on my website on many of the topics of my book including what technology is recommended. Remember, I've put together a free resources page for you that you can access anytime as you read through this book. It's good to do this too because technology changes and since the book is already written, I have to update this resources page for you if things change, not the book.

www.JumpstartYourBizNow.com/JumpstartBookResources

Product Images

You want to be very careful with images these days. Most of the images you Google or find online, even on Facebook and other sites are copyrighted and not yours to use freely. You could get sued if found using them!

Let's be clear, you have to either develop your own images, meaning design them yourself, or you should

Online Set-Up

pay for images to use on your website and your marketing.

Don't just use anything you find or you'll be subject to being sued. I got sued early on in my business because I used to take fun graphics and pictures off Google and put them on my webpages and blog posts. I didn't know what I didn't know but even with an attorney, I couldn't get out of paying a $1,000 fine for each image at that time.

There are many sites that you can subscribe to for a small fee or sometimes for free and you can create your own images for your website, social media, blogs and even your logo. Canva.com is the main one I and countless others use these days. I highly recommend paying the $12.99 fee that they charge (current pricing) to be able to use and create basically any image or graphic your company will ever need.

Trust me, this is a very affordable way to have fun graphics for your marketing, your website, your entire business even. I use Canva exclusively now. I used to pay a graphic designer hundreds of dollars for basic materials, and now I do it all for free myself or pay my $8/hour Virtual Assistant to do for me in my Canva account.

As far as your logo goes, while branding is important like I said, I recommend not spending a lot of money on your logo or too much branding and design until you've gone a year into your business. Typically, your focus changes in our business within that first year. You also get a lot more clarity on who you work with and what you do.

Besides, no one really cares about your logo, trust me. The first few years of your business there are plenty of other things that you need to invest money in that are more important for sales and marketing than a logo.

Branding could be the graphic design part of it all or it could mean the messaging of it all. The messaging is much more important to get down early on in your business than the graphics.

Both are important for positioning, however. Positioning goes way beyond the design. Positioning, to me, is what you look like from the outside looking in. For a new prospect or referral source, when they first get introduced to you, what are they going to do?

Look at your website, look at your social media profiles or at least one of them perhaps, and they're going to judge you based on what you look like in those places and also perhaps if they met you in person, or on a Zoom call, what you looked like showing up at that event.

- Do you look like an expert?
- Do you look like someone who would make a great speaker at their next conference?
- Do you look like someone who could charge $20,000 for a program?

EXERCISE: Take a good look at what YOU look like on the outside looking in for someone who's never met you before. Evaluate yourself, your branding, positioning and expert status.

Is it clear that you know what you're doing, or do you look like an amateur with a GoDaddy self-made website? Do you look like an expert with professional clothes, photos, Zoom room set up or do you look like you just came in from the gym online and your photos are fuzzy, like your cat took them?

Email Marketing & Follow Up

Many people ask me what the difference is between an email blast, broadcast or newsletter and an autoresponder.

Basically, the difference is that an email blast, broadcast or newsletter is typically created then sent at that moment in time or you can schedule it out. For example, if you wanted to write one email newsletter per week but you were headed on vacation later in the month, you might pre-write your newsletter for the week you're going to be gone, and then schedule it to send via your software during your vacation.

An autoresponder is pre-written and left to be sent once a website visitor takes an action. You can pre-write and schedule autoresponders and broadcasts if you're using a shopping cart or email system that allows for that.

Autoresponders allow for you to continually be following up with new prospects or clients while you're not there. You can set it and forget it and then the series of emails that you've prewritten will be send to the individuals one by one according to the schedule you've set them up to go.

If you didn't want to be stuck writing a regular email or newsletter to those who sign up on your list regularly, then you could write a series of two to 26 tips or pieces of content at one time and schedule them out in an autoresponder to cover a 6-month or one-year period.

Online Set-Up

I do recommend whatever your email strategy is that you email them a minimum of twice a month. Weekly however, is much better. I have friends sending emails daily and seeing great results. Whatever you decide your strategy is, don't base it on what you like or don't like, however. Do what is necessary to run and grow your business please.

What do you put in your emails? Content, some type of useable content.

As a marketer, you should constantly be creating content. Block time on your calendar to create content even if it's just 20 minutes once a week. Write something or record something, it doesn't matter. Don't worry about doing what "they say" whoever you're listening to. I say: Do whatever is easiest for you.

Here is a graphic depicting a few common database marketing strategies, especially those for retainment or creating a wow customer experience.

Jumpstart Your New Business Now!

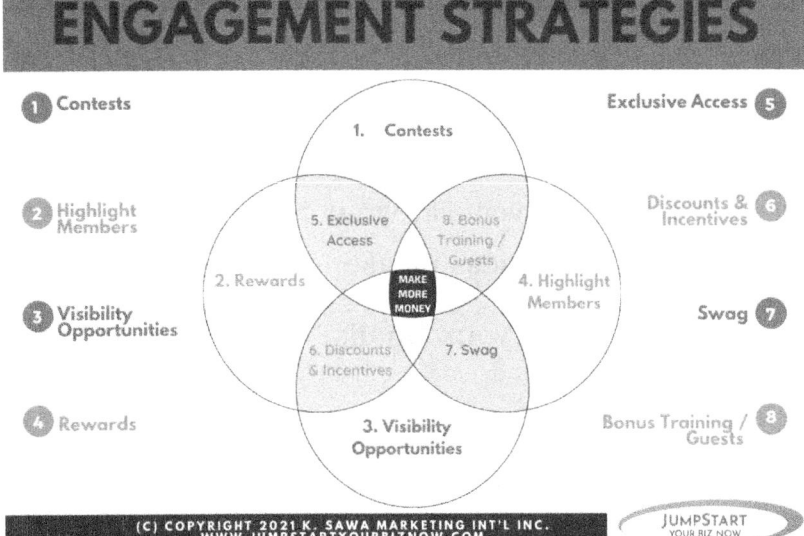

What additional systems, services or software could you need?

- Website Hosting Company
- Business Bank Account
- Webinar software
- Text message software
- Graphic and/or Website Designer
- Virtual Assistants
- Search Engine Optimization Company or Systems
- Printer

Online Set-Up

- Birthday or Greeting card sending service
- Direct Mail House
- Video Camera/Web Cam/Videographer
- Lighting and good microphone for virtual calls and podcasting
- Photo or clip art site
- Membership/Forum software
- Online Data Backup System
- Remote Access Software
- Copywriter
- YouTube Channel
- Social media platforms and profiles

There could be so many other systems that could help you be more efficient, make more sales and run your business smoother so you don't have to work so hard. But you may not know what you don't know. And I wouldn't know what to share with you unless we could have a conversation which I highly recommend as a next step for you after reading this book.

Jumpstart Your New Business Now!

I urge you to get some training around your business development, marketing, sales and foundational systems. I can help you. But you have to realize you need some help and you have to reach out and ask for it. Remember, you are not supposed to know all of this. All of this I had to learn over time myself. I've paid mentors, taken courses, joined memberships, masterminds, attended workshops and seminars – all of it. I still do, 21 years into my business because I still don't know what I don't know, and I am constantly looking to take my business to the next level.

Please make sure you access that book resources page that I put together for you and consider either grabbing one of my online trainings to hone your skills around a number of these topics in this book. They are all listed and available here: www.JumpstartYourBizNow.com/trainings.

You can also come speak with me. Schedule a call at www.AskKat.biz.

"3 SIMPLE STEPS TO ATTRACTING CLIENTS: 1) GET IN FRONT OF MORE PEOPLE 2) MAKE IT EASY TO BUY 3) UTILIZE A PROVEN FOLLOW UP SYSTEM." ~ KATRINA SAWA

Chapter 11

Relationship Marketing

"You need to reach out to at least 1,000 NEW prospects and people every single month."
*~ **Katrina Sawa***

The most important area you need to learn and stay informed about besides sales, are the marketing basics that will drive more traffic to your website and more clients to you.

There are over 20 marketing strategies that I teach to clients and in my programs. We don't have the bandwidth to go into them in-depth here nor do you have to do all 20 in your business.

Let me share an overview with you about how I look at marketing and lead generation.

There are basically 3 types of marketing:

1. New business marketing
2. Database marketing

3. Referral source marketing

Most of the activities that you'll do will fall into one of those three categories.

The difference is basically the messaging you use. You won't want to say the same thing to a new prospect, someone who doesn't know you, as you do to someone who already knows you and has been following you or your emails.

It's important to be very clear on your marketing plan so you can focus your time and money on what will work for YOUR business.

How much marketing you need to do depends on the amount of people you really need to come in contact with every month in order to have enough people to sell effectively into your programs, products and services.

So, it's mass marketing, but it's not necessarily cold calling or impersonal marketing. With technology, you can, in fact, reach over 1,000 new potential clients every single month. That used to be the number of new people I would suggest people get in front of each month in order to make the money they want to make. It's a numbers game. It still is.

Relationship Marketing

In 1996, I took a job doing door-to-door sales. I was told by my boss to knock on 100 doors a day and I would make 10 sales which was my goal. That accounted for all the homes where no one was home as well as those who were who wouldn't buy.

I learned sales strategies that year and beyond from two of the greats, Zig Ziglar and Brian Tracy.

When I followed that rule, I would 99% of the time make my 10, or more, sales. When I goofed off or left early for the day, I would never make my goal.

This is what I want you to remember about marketing in your business. It's the consistent CEO who sells, grows and scales. And don't worry, you don't have to do door-to-door sales if you don't want to! (Unless you're a landscaping company, I highly recommend it then!)

Unfortunately, these days, people are getting hit with marketing messages and inbox messages from so many different sources that they're overwhelmed and ignoring much of them unlike before.

The number one thing I always tell clients about marketing first, however, is that you never ever, ever, ever want to base your own marketing strategies of what you're going to do to promote your business and get clients on what you like or don't like being done to you.

That means, if you don't like it when someone emails you every other day or every week, you can't decide to just not send emails. You need to send emails.

Or if you don't like to get direct mail or don't like to get phone calls or don't like to be connected to a stranger on Facebook that doesn't necessarily mean you shouldn't go do it. All of these strategies work for the right kind of business with the right messaging.

Now, if you don't like attending networking events or you don't like speaking, that's a little different. We can get you more comfortable with those or perhaps avoid those to a certain extent. These strategies are more personal though and can't really be delegated. They also happen to be the #1 and #2 most effective ways to get clients. I would not avoid these strategies.

The first type of marketing is new business marketing.

New business marketing is going after your ideal target client wherever they may be. This is attracting or targeting people you don't know.

The top five ways of finding new business is via:

Relationship Marketing

- Live events either with networking, exhibiting, sponsoring or speaking
- Virtual events, summits, speaking gigs, including podcasts, webinars and even live social broadcasts
- Social media connecting
- Direct mail and cold calling (for some)
- Publicity, getting interviewed on TV or in print media and more

The second type of marketing is database marketing.

Database marketing is the nurturing and relationship building that you do with and to the people who already know you. Whether they've decided to like and trust you yet is a different story.

The messages for database marketing connections are usually more relationship oriented. You know, "hey it's Katrina again I wanted to let you know about this."

You can talk with them as you know them and they know you. If they didn't like it or you, they would go away.

The top five ways of marketing to your database is via:

- Email marketing
- Videos that you share with subscribers or with those who follow you
- Phone calls
- Direct mail
- Connecting with connections, clients and followers on social sites

Database marketing for me though, includes everyone and anyone you know or have access to. So, I extend this relationship building strategy into those you know via:

- Organizations you belong to and the members within
- Social media groups you belong to where there is a common ground
- People in your past, such as high school or previous job colleagues
- Friends of friends, people in your circle of influence that know of you

- Even your professional connections like your dentist, therapist, or dry cleaner – you never know where your next client or referral may come from

The third type of marketing is referral source marketing.

Referral source marketing is obviously all about referrals. It could be people that are in your database already or it could be groups of people or individuals that you can ask or seek out to support you that you may not yet know.

You want to look at everybody that you currently have access to and determine which of them are more likely and eager to refer you.

- It could be an individual that you know who follows you online

- It could be a client that really loves you and likes to refer you to their friends

- It could be an organization that is full of your ideal target clients who lets you speak for their meetings

- It could be a type of industry like chiropractors for example make a great referral source for massage therapists

When speaking with or to a referral source, you want to hit the hot buttons of the referral source, not their clients. Sometimes referral sources are motivated by referral commissions, more often though, they just want their referrals taken care of.

The top six ways of marketing to referral sources and finding new referral sources is via:

- Segmenting in your email list and reaching out often via email
- Phone calls
- Direct mail
- Live networking events
- Interviewing them or being interviewed by them – either on a podcast, webinar, or Live Broadcast
- Connecting with them on social media

Keep in mind that marketing to referral sources cuts down on the number of people you have to market to because if you can get in front of someone else's list

Relationship Marketing

it's faster to reach more people than doing it one-on-one.

I wish I had time to go into depth in this book about all the different ways you can market yourself but again, it would be 500 pages!

I do have a Jumpstart Your Marketing Training on my website. Please go take advantage of something else over there to get you more training on the marketing. This part is critical to your success.

Which marketing strategies you choose depends on your business, your goals, your prospects and what you're selling.

How to know what to do and how?

Jumpstart Your New Business Now!

Jumpstart Your Marketing!

Here's a chart with a huge list of strategies.

It's all about what to focus on day after day and how to simplify what you're doing so that what really needs to get done actually does get done.

I have a 3-step system for attracting clients:

1. Getting in front of more people more often and in more ways

2. Make it easier for people to buy (or get info)

3. Implement an interactive relationship marketing follow up system

Relationship Marketing

It's pretty simple. But going to a couple networking events a month and making a few friends on Facebook won't cut it, it won't be enough. You have to put the right marketing plan and system into place to reach a lot more people than this to make a lot more money doing what you love.

Granted if you created a cool video that a lot of people shared, it could go viral. Videos can go viral pretty quickly. But that's also not a realistic expectation.

Yes, if you had a friend who had a really big email list, and they promoted you to their list, you could get a ton of new subscribers and paying customers really quick.

If you build a great following on social media and everyone online loves your posts and they engage with you often, it's very possible that you could promote something to them to make you a lot of money.

Yes, all those things have come true before.

Are they the norm? No.

Will you need to do a lot of different types of marketing to build the business of your dreams? Yes, most likely for 99% of you.

Owning your own business isn't easy but it doesn't have to be hard either.

I've gotten help over the years, and you can too.

Making it Easy to Buy

This has a lot to do with being prepared offline and online, on your website.

On your website, your visitors and prospects need to be able to do the following:

- Understand immediately what your site is about
- Find what they're looking for
- Engage by filling in a form or clicking for info
- Realize that you're speaking to them
- Understand that you get them
- Get the facts or learn more
- Get on your list so you can continue to market to them and follow up

Make it easier for people to buy or get information from you offline by:

- Bringing information with you
- Have enough business cards

Relationship Marketing

- Get a name tag for yourself

- Put a sign on your car with your phone number, logo and your website

- Bring order forms or flyers with you

- Be prepared to ask for the sale and take money

- Have an initial offer that people can sign up for when they see you in person

- Grab their contact information so you can follow up, don't just give them yours because they won't

Step number three is really making sure that you have a comprehensive follow up system in place so that no one falls through the cracks after all of these lead generation activities.

You can get access to my free follow up audio training and flowchart on that special resources page I mentioned here:

www.JumpstartYourBizNow.com/JumpstartBookResources

Jumpstart Your New Business Now!

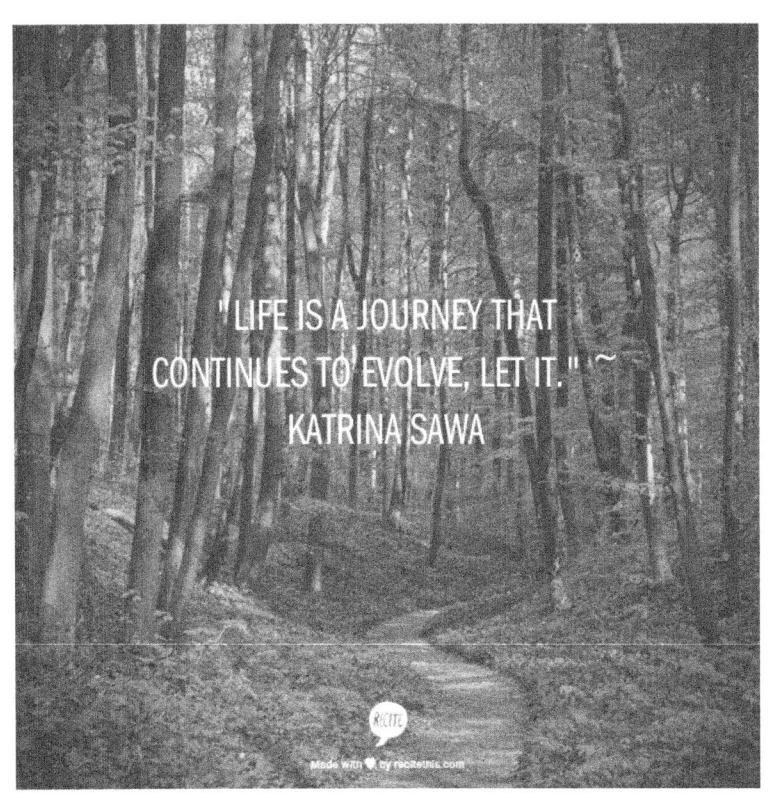

Chapter 12

Team Building

"You want to build a team for more freedom!"
*~ **Katrina Sawa***

The reason I'm talking about team building is because team building equals freedom. You want to build the business around the kind of life you want to live?

Then you need a team.

Small or large, the people you do hire will be critical to you being able to take time off, go on vacation and to reach a lot more people with your message.

You want to know how and when to build your team and support system or how to upgrade the team you've got if you already have one.

You might be looking at your checkbook balance asking yourself, "How am I going to pay an assistant if I can't even pay myself enough yet?"

Well, you don't have to hire someone full time. You hire part time employees if you need to, otherwise most of us just hire independent contractors. Typically that means in this day and age, you hire a Virtual Assistant.

However Virtual Assistants, or VAs, are not created equal. Many are well trained but some just start up a business not really knowing their skills or how to run a business. Be careful who you hire.

I actually started with a bookkeeper first. That was the thing that was not getting done the most in my business within its first couple years.

The thing that prompted me to hire a bookkeeper first was that by month nine in my business I had to do my taxes, and in order to do my taxes, I had to know my numbers, and my expenses, etc. Well, I had no idea what I was doing with all of that.

My mom knew how to do this, and I asked her to show me, she helped me and did it for me basically but then said she wasn't coming back so I needed to hire someone from there on out!

Then I hired an assistant to work in my home office a couple hours a week. I found out though, that I was

Team Building

very bad at micromanaging, especially with someone in my space like that.

I realized that I was a control freak. You might be also?

It's ok, many entrepreneurs are, but the successful ones are the ones that get over that and let stuff go.

I also thought that person would "Learn by Osmosis" what I needed them to do. That was not an effective leadership strategy as you can imagine. I had to learn how to train people too, regardless of if I wanted to or not.

I gradually delegated more and more as the years went on, realizing the more I got off my plate, the higher my revenues climbed.

I also hired local or Americans at first, meeting people along the way at events who said they could help me, or taking referrals from friends. But I started paying pretty high rates, up to $60-85/hour for some people. It adds up if you don't look around, do your due diligence and really vet a good person or team.

By delegating more though, I was able to focus on more revenue generating activities. You can also if you just get started.

Where do you start?

Start with the tasks you dislike doing the most or aren't really good at doing.

Don't just look at your professional tasks for what needs to be outsourced. Also look to your personal and household tasks such as hiring a housekeeper, landscaper, personal chef or trainer.

When do you know you are ready to expand your team?

Always be on the lookout for the things that are bogging you down. Also, be aware of what you're avoiding but should be doing!

If you have an assistant who does more administrative work for you such as filing, invoicing, phone calls, customer service and direct mail for example, you may at some point also require the support of someone more technology minded.

Techy tasks are what I hire out more for these days and my clients are the same. There's just too much to know about, learn and implement online for us to be able to figure it all out ourselves. You want to stick to what you do best and leave those types of tasks to the people who are good at them.

And finally, part of your team should involve your support professionals such as:

Team Building

- Attorneys – Business, Intellectual Property and Trust
- CPA / Accountant
- Bookkeepers
- Insurance
- Financial planner
- Coach / Mentors
- Graphic designers
- Website designers

You may not need all of these folks often but when you need them you need them now.

Exercise: Write down everything that you're doing for an entire week, business and personal tasks.

You will be amazed at where you're wasting time. You'll also be amazed at things that are not on the list that you know need to be on the list.

Then sort those tasks to which ones you truly need to be doing and which can be delegated. Then determine (if you're able) which types of people or support you really need to take some of those off your plate. There is a great tool for this on the book resources page, go grab it!

www.JumpstartYourBizNow.com/JumpstartBookResources

Now, you will have to embrace the idea that it's OK if something doesn't get done as good as you would have done it, at least at first. Give your new team time to get in the groove and do their thing. If you give up too early on, you will never design that dream business you so deeply want.

Learn to manage and run your team with effective leadership qualities. Hold weekly meetings to start to establish best working relationships and expectations.

In order to overcome being a control freak, you've got to know what's more important. What's more important is your big picture vision, your goals and accomplishing your goals.

Know that the end result of being more successful and making more money relies on you running this business like a CEO, thinking logically and being clear and focused.

Team Building

Chapter 13

Advanced Strategies

"It's important to build your business while implementing strategies <u>in order of importance.</u>"
~ Katrina Sawa

So, what's next for you once the basic business is set up and you've got a few clients coming in?

Well, it depends... you can add more business models, raise your rates, uplevel your exposure online and do a lot more marketing to reach a lot more people.

Some entrepreneurs think in terms of hosting their own events now or writing a book and becoming an author.

Those are great strategies to do but you do typically want to wait a bit, at least until you have some consistent revenues coming in to launch into those strategies.

You want to make sure your relationship marketing and follow up system doesn't have any holes in it and is working to bring in and convert leads.

If the basic marketing and business strategies and systems are not in place yet or not working properly then my advice is to not necessarily move on to any advanced strategies yet or you'll be spreading yourself too thin.

Advanced strategies could include but not be limited to things such as:

- Developing your signature system
- Creating online products
- Running a group program or mastermind
- Membership programs
- Becoming an author
- Speaking more or selling from stage
- Hosting your own live event or retreat
- Becoming a podcast or radio show host
- Hosting an online summit
- Getting publicity
- Facebook or other online advertising

- Spending money for SEO advertising

Speaking to grow your business

Speaking is one of the more advanced strategies that I do believe you should start on early on. Just don't expect to make big speaking fees right off the bat if you're new.

You want to speak for free like I discussed earlier on in the book, to get leads and clients. If you're not good yet at selling from stage or from a webinar, then drive people to a free consult with you where you can sell them into something.

Speaking as a guest on podcasts or radio shows is good though. Although podcasting has gotten a lot more professional than back in the day of calling into a conference line which is how I hosted my own radio show on BlogTalkRadio a long time ago.

Podcast hosts want to bring in guests that look good, sound good and have great interview skills. This is something you can definitely learn and practice with now.

Besides speaking, which I think everyone should do as soon as possible, becoming an author is one I would push you into adding sooner than later.

Becoming an author

When to know you're ready to become an author?

If you need the business to bring in money in order to survive and pay the bills, then it's probably not time to write a FULL book just yet. It's very difficult to do both.

However, it could be relatively easy and less expensive to write a chapter in a compilation book. That's how I got started writing books. I was too busy back in 2006 to write my own full book, as I was building my client base and consistent revenues. It was, however, very easy to write a long blog post or chapter for a book that someone else was publishing. It was a great collaboration with 20 other entrepreneurs that really catapulted me and my business back then.

So much so that I did another compilation book, and a third one too before I wrote my first full book, Love Yourself Successful. Even that full book, then took me 3 years to get out of me and finalize. If I'd waited on me to just write that first full book before becoming an author, it would have been 6 more years!

Advanced Strategies

If you do have a relatively consistent business now, or money coming in, and you're ready to write your own book, I say do it!

If you don't know what to write about or how to write a book and it's not coming out of you, you can always hire someone to write the book. People will interview you and pull it out of you or they can ghostwrite it.

I know what a huge difference being an author has made in my business.

Being an author has helped me:

- Become the expert in my industry
- Become well known
- Get more speaking gigs
- Get free publicity on TV
- Do joint ventures with referral sources
- Increase my confidence
- Given me curriculum from which to teach and hold events around
- Become an authority
- And so much more!

It's an interesting process writing a book I must say. I actually took a book writing course before I wrote my book and it wasn't to figure out how to write the book. I knew that that would come to me. It was about what to do around the book, how to market the book and what I needed to know before I wrote the book.

The positioning of your book within your business and how it will help you sell other programs, products and services is actually one of the most important parts about becoming an author that people forget.

Advanced Strategies

They just start writing a book but they don't think of how it's going to intersect with the entire business.

You don't just want to have a book to have a book and then nobody read it because you didn't market it because you don't know what you're doing with your book.

This is why it's important not to have to worry about paying the bills when you start out with this strategy.

When my first full book came out in 2012, I hired a publisher to help me get it done and out. It was $6,000 just for basic editing, cover design and publishing. No Amazon best-seller campaign or coaching. But I didn't know what I didn't know back then and needed someone who knew what to do to handle it.

When this book that you're reading now originally came out in 2018, I had no idea how the publishing world worked, but I learned that it would be easier and less expensive to publish it if I learned how to do it myself.

So, I hired a couple of my publishing friends to show me how it all worked, what to do, etc. I found some great vendors and online services for authors that made it more affordable, and I got this first book published for under $1,000!

These days, I have a full-service publishing company called Jumpstart Publishing. I help authors like me who need some help and/or those who want to learn how, and those who want to get it done the most affordable way possible. We offer everything you need at a la carte pricing. Check out what we do and offer online at www.JumpstartPublishing.net.

Hosting Events

Hosting your own live events is also a very cool strategy to do once you have a good amount of people on your list. Until you do, it will be a little more difficult to get a bunch of them to attend. If you have 500 people on your email list for example, don't think that 100 of them will show up. You'll be lucky to get 5 of them realistically.

If you get more, great but I want you to spend your time and money wisely on what to do first, second and third here.

Advanced Strategies

Chapter 14

What's Next?

"You want to be open to the evolution of you and your business; you and it are never done."
~ Katrina Sawa

You may not be thinking about what's next for you after reading this since I've given you a bunch of things to get started doing.

The reality is however that most entrepreneurs fail. Most go out of business because they don't learn how to run a consistent, moneymaking business.

Most don't get or seek the help and mentors that can support them and get them where they need to go next or tell them what to do when.

I do.

I am more than just a business coach. As one of my clients Alicia says, "I'm a mentor and a friend too." I get you. I get where you are. I understand where you want to go and what type of lifestyle you want to create for yourself, and I can guide you directly and exactly along the way.

I know the struggles you've been through and will go through and how to help you navigate around them for the least amount of damage.

You can trust me with your business, I won't steer you wrong.

My goal remember, is to help people like you create happier lives for yourself. I do that by helping you learn how to make a lot more money doing what you love!

I hired mentors to help me get where I am.

Let me help you get where you want to go.

I will show you the way, give you the roadmap, guide you and hold you accountable along the way so you don't stop short of your dreams.

You can do this with my help.

Everyone needs a mentor and coach. I'm the perfect one for you now if you need the basics set up in your business and you want to do it the right way from the start.

I'm the perfect mentor for you if you've started already but aren't making enough money yet and you

What's Next?

have to figure this out quick or you might have to go back and get a JOB.

I'm the perfect mentor for you if you've tried other programs and they haven't worked. I cover a LOT more than other coaches out there when it comes to marketing, systems and creating more consistent cash flow.

And I'm the perfect mentor for you if you want to get to the next level in your business and life and you're highly motivated to do what it takes, go ALL IN and create it now.

Don't deny yourself the success you're seeking and that you deserve.

Don't let your fears and doubts get in the way...

Don't let other naysayers in your life hold you back either, you deserve more. Come to a call with me today to see if I'm a good fit for you just as I'll see if you're a good fit for me.

→ Sign up here now: http://www.AskKat.biz

About Katrina Sawa

The Jumpstart Your Biz Coach International Speaker and 13x Int'l Best-Selling Author

Katrina Sawa is known as the JumpStart Your Biz Coach because she literally kicks her clients and their businesses into high gear, online & offline, and fast.

Katrina is the creator of the Jumpstart Your Marketing & Sales System, Jumpstart Your Business in 90 Days System, and Jumpstart Yourself as a Speaker System. She is the author of 20 other books including *Love Yourself Successful, Power and Soul* with Ali Brown, *Entrepreneur Success Stories* with Loral Langemeier and *Success Rituals 2.0* with a variety of other online marketers. Katrina's anthology

book series, *Jumpstart Your* _____ (blank), where authors write chapters on what they help people jumpstart, has published 80 authors in six books and all the books in this series have attained international best-seller status since 2018.

Katrina helps entrepreneurs make smarter marketing and business decisions in order to create the life and business of your dreams. She helps you create your big picture vision, plan and initial offerings if you're just starting out.

Kat helps you develop a more leveraged, efficient business and marketing plan if you're more seasoned. Either way, she shows you all the steps, systems and marketing that need to be put in place in order to accomplish your big picture business, life and money goals.

One thing that makes Katrina different is that she also focuses on your personal life. She found that most business owners lack enough self-confidence to truly enable them to get to their next level or take those leaps of faith they need to take to finally achieve their ultimate dreams. Katrina's goal is to inspire, motivate and educate entrepreneurs how to love yourself fully, live a bigger life and leverage yourself to complete happiness.

About the Author

Katrina has a degree in Business Administration, Marketing Concentration from California State University Sacramento and has been a featured business expert on three of her local television news channels throughout her career thus far as well as hundreds of other publications, media, and podcasts.

Katrina lives in Northern California with her husband Jason, stepdaughter Riley and their loving dog Luna. She gives back to her community, speaks all over the world in person and virtually and she is very accessible to her clients with many options for getting the support you need.

Jumpstart Your New Business Now!

You can find out all about Kat and her products, programs, services and live events online at:

www.JumpstartYourBizNow.com and

www.JumpstartPublishing.net.

About the Author

What others are saying about Katrina Sawa and her strategies:

"If you are looking for a good coach/mentor who really cares about you and your business, and not just taking your money, I have been working with Katrina Sawa for about 10 months now and can say she is a fantastic coach. She has a great mind for marketing and developing your business. I encourage you to attend one of her events and see for yourself just how amazing she is!" - Angela Hall, That Helpful Chick Techy Services

"I got a ton out of your coaching. Many times, with coaches, it's just the same old ideas re-used 10 years later. I have enough material to implement from the next several months." - Robert Plank, Podcaster, Internet Marketer

"For over three years, Katrina's coaching has increased my confidence as a business owner, productivity and sales. I now earn more than I ever dreamed, and her marketing strategies do produce real results and it's why I recommend her coaching services to colleagues and my own clients." - Alicia White, Brand Strategist

"One of Katrina's strengths is that she has the systems you need to automate your business with ease. From sales scripts to social media marketing plans, to email marketing guides, she has it all figured out for you." - Jennifer Darling, Sales Coach

"I decided to work with Katrina after her 3-day event, even though I went to the event with no intention of hiring a coach. I liked her business knowledge and her desire to help her clients succeed in their business. I have found while working with her for the last year, I continue to learn an incredible amount. She is constantly learning the latest business techniques and she freely gives this knowledge to her clients. My confidence has increased substantially since I have worked with Katrina, and I consistently stretch out of my comfort zone. My business has transformed in ways I could have never imagined, and she continues to help me with new ideas." - Kim McLaughlin, MA

"Katrina is a master at internet marketing. It was Katrina that introduce me to having a business that can be global and mobile. She gave me the tools to launch and build my online empire." - Dorris Burch

About the Author

"I worked with Katrina to help me create the first of many info products and to truly jump start my marketing. From the moment we began our coaching session, I knew I was working with a consummate professional who understood exactly what I needed to help develop a successful business." - Jonathon Aslay

"Katrina is serious and fun when it comes to helping you zero in on your business model and structure. She's got a knack for finding possible streams of income that you can start building and implementing right away. I also find her to be honest and upfront about her own business experiences which is so refreshing." - Helen Kim, Money Mentor

"I learned so much about marketing, websites and advertising; I see that she has a focused, well-thought-out plan for my business that will aid me in achieving my goals. Her dynamic, enthusiastic approach speaks not only to her broad understanding of how to best help her clients, but also to her kind, caring nature." - David Greenwood, Greenwood Hypnosis & Wellness Center

"Katrina tells you exactly what you need to do to build a successful business." - Leslie Ellis, Savvy Selling Now

Jumpstart Your New Business Now!

"It was so wonderful to speak with someone who was so knowledgeable and who "got" my business. I was amazed at how much material we covered and all the ideas I had to implement in my marketing." - Lisa O'Dell-Nin, Virtual Assistant

"Katrina helped me get focused with an action plan and defined goals. Plain and simple, saying that my experience with Katrina was "worth it", does not nearly do it justice." ~ Kevin Harris

"Within our first session, Katrina provided me with the information that I needed to begin transforming my website to more clearly express the value that I offer through my work and then strategies to increase my visitor rate and client interest." - Lisa Hromada, Branding Expert

"Katrina Sawa is the real deal! Marketing secrets that I've heard from no one else, and practical spot-on, step-by-step advice flows from her like it's channeled from a higher power!" - Wendy Vineyard, Menopause Coach

About the Author

Grab One or More of the Jumpstart Your Business Free Trainings Now!

Learn How to:

- Get Started Speaking
- Jumpstart Your Business
- Implement Best Marketing Practices
- Build an Effective
- Website
- Create a Life You Love
- Find Your Purpose
- Love Yourself Successful
- Delegate & Build Your Team
- And more!

Get Access Online at:
www.JumpstartYourBizNow.com/FreeTrainings

Take the Jumpstart Your Biz Quiz to Find What's MISSING in Your Business too!

www.JumpstartYourBizQuiz.com

Additional Trainings Available Online Include:

Jumpstart Your Marketing

Jumpstart Your Networking

Jumpstart Your Sales

Jumpstart Your Online Course

Jumpstart Your Events

Big Picture Business Planning

Pricing for Profits

Delegating for Freedom

Technology & Systems

Authentically Speaking

For Info & Access, go to:
www.JumpstartYourBizNow.com/trainings

Pick Up One of Kat's Other Books!

"*Love Yourself Successful* is a compassionate and much-needed guide for any woman who dares to be successful, happy, and of service to the world. Katrina weaves clearly-defined action steps and practices with heartfelt personal examples to help you move beyond your comfort zone and into a life of greater, richer possibility." **– Ali Brown, the Entrepreneurial Guru for Women**

Grab Copies of Any Books at:
www.JumpstartBookstore.com

Attend One of Kat's Live Events! Get Info at:

www.JumpstartEvents.net

If You're Ready to Really Live BIG & Create the Business & Life of Your Dreams...

Then you want to join Kat's...

Jumpstart Your Next Level Mastermind!

Motivate and Inspire Others!

"Share this Book"

Retail $16.95 + Tax & Shipping

Special Quantity Discounts

5 - 15 Books	$11.95 Each
16 - 30 Books	$9.95 Each
30 - 1,000 Books	$7.95 Each

To Place an Order Contact:

K. Sawa Marketing International Inc.

916-872-4000

info@JumpstartYourBizNow.com or go to
www.JumpstartYourBizNow.com/orderbooks

The Ideal Speaker for Your Next Event!

Any organization that wants to help their small business or entrepreneur audiences to become more profitable in their businesses needs to hire Katrina for a keynote and/or workshop training!

To Contact or Book Katrina to Speak:

K. Sawa Marketing International Inc.

PO Box 6

Roseville, CA 95661

916-872-4000

info@jumpstartyourbiznow.com

www.JumpstartYourBizNow.com/speaking

Made in the USA
Monee, IL
27 September 2023

43566166R00125